THE WOKE WRITER

A Companion For The
Conscious Muslim Woman Writer

By Aishah Alam

The Woke Writer | A Companion For The Conscious Muslim Woman Writer

Published by Strange Inc, a nonprofit publishing house based in New York. Our mission is to elevate the authentic voices of Muslim women.

Email: hello@strangeincorporated.org

Website: www.strangeincorporated.org

Phone: +1 (347) 560-8334

ISBN: ebook 979-8-9855898-9-4

ISBN: Paperback 979-8-9855898-7-0

ISBN: Hardback 979-8-9855898-8-7

Cover Design by Alexandra Sieh

Interior Design by Alexandra Sieh

Edited by Laura El Alam

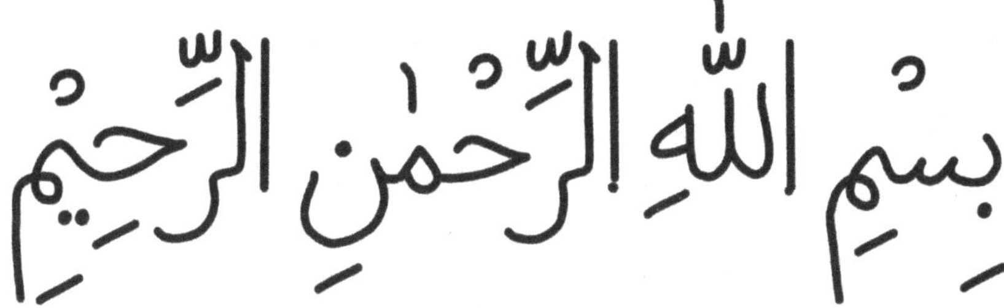

بِسْمِ اللهِ الرَّحْمٰنِ الرَّحِيمِ

CONTENTS

INTRODUCTION

I want to thank you for being here with me. For opening these pages and wanting to use these words to learn more about yourself.

As women, we are known for being mothers and wives. As writers we are known for our inspiration and creativity. As Muslims we are known for our faith and obedience to Allah, and as humans we are known for our triumphs and defeats. It feels like there are so many parts of us, and sometimes it can be difficult to reconcile them. How can we be faithful Muslims, good mothers, *and* take writing seriously? Does it make me a bad person when I choose to write instead of doing something else — anything else? Why do I feel so guilty writing? I'm here to tell you that yes, we have many facets, but we are a whole being, and it is important to embrace the parts of us that make us feel complete. But how can we pursue our passion for writing without it conflicting with our worship of Allah?

I wondered about that too, and my answer came from a direction I never would have expected. It came with this need to learn about intuition, a theme that has since become central to this book. My initial curiosity quickly turned into confusion as I delved deeper into my research on the subject. I listened to podcasts, read articles and books, but instead of feeling more connected to my intuition, I felt lost and disconnected from myself.

I had so many questions, like: "What does it mean when I'm thinking about chocolate cake and then I see it on the billboard in a subway? (And I'm on a sugar cleanse)." "What does it mean when my two year old is jumping on my lap just as I sit down to write extra early? Should I just stop? Is this a block?" And then my questions became broader, like: "What does intuition have to do with writing? *Is* it inspiration?" "Do Muslims even believe that inspiration has a place in our lives?" "What have the scholars of Islam said about it?" I decided then to reach out to a trusted person of knowledge whom I consider a teacher and ask him for resources. Dr. Hatem Al Haj sent me his lectures on various topics related to inspiration, and as I listened to them, the vagueness of intuition became clearer. I now had a grasp of the concept that I could use in my everyday life with confidence, and it felt like for the first time, a treasure of ease came upon me in a way that only true knowledge can give.

After that, I deepened my research into intuition and found that it was not only a spiritual thing, but a whole-body connection. It was affected by trauma, our own biases, outside forces, and so much more. With all this knowledge, I decided to go back to the basics of what our ultimate purpose — our Big Why — is. And that is when I had a wow moment: Everything is connected to our Big Why and to the very foundation of our belief in the oneness of Allah.

Once I had gathered my research, Imam John Starling looked over the information for authenticity in accordance with the Quran and the Sunnah. Then Strange Inc., our nonprofit publishing house, launched the companion video course to this book: *The Woke Writer.*

What I love about Islam is that it encompasses every part of us, and when we are living our purpose — to worship Allah — every single part of us becomes aligned. It is through that alignment that our writing will follow suit, and it is with this approach that you and I will meet one another through this book. My hope is that by the end of this book, your vision as a Muslim woman and a writer will be brought to life with renewed energy, empowering you to shape a new and beautiful world through your words.

My lovely sister, there are so many forces opposing our highest purpose, and it can become easy to lose sight of what truly matters. It is time that we own the parts of us that are unique, deep, creative, and visionary. Everything we create has the power to reflect the best of us, and I pray this book will be a comforting companion, guiding you on your journey towards becoming the best version of your most authentic self.

HOW TO MAKE THE MOST OF THIS BOOK

I will share everything you need to know about being *Woke*, which means to be conscious in every part of our internal and external lives. It is to be intentional. To be present. To live our Big Why which is our ultimate purpose. The reason why we were placed on this Earth, which is to worship our Lord. To be Woke is it to embrace our Small Why — the *how* to our Big Why. It is where every fiber of our being works as one, united in growth with a goal of true greatness, headed by love for Allah, so from the moment our eyes wake up in the morning, as our limbs ask us to do good for the day, we listen. We appreciate. Where every step we take is an act of worship. Where every word we write is part of our Big Why. Woke means to be awakened to the true self, in accordance with the Quran and the Sunnah of our Prophet Muhammed ﷺ. And as we become an embodiment of the Woke woman, it is then we shall create our greatest masterpiece as a writer.

To make the most of your experience in reading this, please try and follow the book in order. I understand that there is a lot of information, and it can be difficult to do everything, so at the end of each chapter, there is only one small thing I have suggested for you to do. As you read, the suggested activities will begin to take form in your life as daily practices and points of reflection. There is also a section for any insights and wow moments. Here, you can share ideas that stood out to you in the chapter. In some of the chapters, I have also added a special space for greatness where you can see the lessons of the chapter in the context of the lives of some of the greatest women in Islam.

This book is divided into four parts:

PART I
THE SOUL

The soul is the foundation of our body, and without it, we simply cannot live. The knowledge shared in this section is fundamental to our whole being; it gives our bodies strength, a fullness and aliveness which cannot be substituted anywhere else. The soul is where a writer's inspiration lives, and with the richness of the soul, all else will follow.

PART II
THE EYES

What enters our eyes affects us. When our lens is polished, everything becomes clear. With this clarity, we will learn the different kinds of inspiration and how we can be blinded from seeing clearly.

PART III
THE VISION

Once we have a firm foundation and our eyes can see clearly, it is time to use our inspiration to bring our visions to life. In this part, we will put all we have learned into action, and I will show writers how to step into their unique creative flow and produce their writing masterpieces. Included in this book is a journal I have created for you to record key information about your writing.

PART IV
LOOK DEEPER

For those of you who want to take things up a notch, I have added a final section full of resources for you to take a deeper look into everything discussed. These resources are also a reference point for the information I have gathered in this book.

I really hope that I can see you on the other end of the book, where I hold a special place of greatness for someone whom I especially want to share with you. Words are powerful, and the words of *Laillaha illAllah,* (there is no God in truth but Allah), weigh heavier on the scales than any others on the Day of Judgement. May Allah guide your hands to write the words you were born to write, and may they weigh heavily on your scales of good on that day. May Allah bless you and give you the ability to grow as a woman, a Muslim, and a writer in alignment with your whole, Woke self. Ameen.

With love and peace,

Your sister Aishah

P.S Grab a preferred beverage, cozy up, and let's get to it!

REGARDING HONORIFICS AND SALUTATIONS

In Islam we honor Allah, His prophets and messengers (particularly Prophet Muhammad ﷺ), and the Prophet's ﷺ Companions with words of praise and blessings. I am using the Arabic glyph ﷺ after the name of our Prophet to honor him, and the translation of these words is "Peace and blessings be upon him."

To ease the flow of the text, I have left out other honorifics and salutations, but I ask the reader to assume the following: for Allah (may He be glorified and exalted). For prophets (peace be upon them), and Companions of the Prophet ﷺ (may Allah be pleased with them).

THE BLUEPRINT TO BEING WOKE

If there is one paragraph you take from this whole book which would summarize all you have learned, this would be it:

The more a servant employs their intellect and acts upon their knowledge and purifies their actions through complete devotion and their conscience becomes purer and they reflect with the sight of intellect, the intelligence of the soul and the acumen of the heart and grow their certainty and abolish their doubts and tame their senses with prophetic etiquettes and reign their thoughts with watchfulness of the divine and avoid lying in speech or action until truthfulness becomes their hometown from which ostentation and self-connectedness are expelled and show need and brokenness before their Lord and disavow their influence and power and commit to service of their Lord and observe the sanctity of proper etiquettes and watch the bounds and adhere to the Sunnah and run away from innovation, the recognition will be elevated and their insight will be sharpened and things hidden from the sights will be disclosed to them and they become the people of lofty rankings by virtue of their gratitude, that results in increase and abundance.[1]

Ibn Taymiyyah

THE BOUNDS OF THE WOKE

The following is a foundation for you to refer to anytime you receive inspiration. For now, you can sweep over them, but in Part II, you will understand their context and why we chose these boundaries as a baseline for anything inspiration-related.

I call this baseline "bounds" because the healthiest boundaries are not rigid or porous. Think of these bounds as a kind of gate around the self in a dangerous world; when the gate is not present, then we either stay too close to our self, unwilling to move forward with life, or we go too far into the danger zone and end up hurting ourselves repeatedly. When that gate around us is clear, we know our place, and within that gate, we have the freedom to truly discover ourselves, without the effect of extremes from outside or inside.

These bounds are gates to your inspiration, and within them, you shall write masterpieces with a fullness of knowledge, wisdom, and humility whilst being guided by the source of the best kind of inspiration, Allah:

ONE | Any Woke hunch is inferior to the revelation of Allah in clarity, certainty, and proof value.

TWO | Our Woke hunches are uncertain and subjective. The testimony of the heart is not enough to be proof of anything.

THREE | Our Woke hunches are exclusive to us. They are not binding on others.

FOUR | Our Woke hunches have a limited scope: they have no place in religious rulings.

THE SOUL

This is the foundation.

The wisdom.

The belief.

The seed.

The thing we return to when we lose everything.

When we have everything.

It is the space where planets orbit,

the roots upon where the tree rises.

You will learn how to be wise.

To grip the beacon of insight

It is the acceptance.

It is the decree.

It is to have power.

And to surrender to The All Powerful,

It is the belief.

Uncorrupted.

Pure.

It is purpose.

This is the meaning of life.

CHAPTER 1

KNOWLEDGE

Knowledge is the basis of growth. It is the offer of guidance, the light which we recognize if our eyes can see, the foundation of the soul if accepted. It is inspiration. A source of motivation. A clarity which gives us strength. The key ingredient of an epiphany when it enters our heart. Knowledge is the map that guides us on our path to our ultimate reason for existence. But all this which I have described is a certain kind of knowledge, purposeful knowledge, that is unseen and bestowed upon us by virtue of being human. Of mattering. Of having our own purpose. In this chapter, I will talk about the different kinds of knowledge and how to recognize the beacon of true knowledge. This is one of the most important chapters in this book, so I ask you to take your time.

Let us begin with the two types of knowledge.

1: APPARENT KNOWLEDGE

We are born with our five senses and through these, we learn to observe the world. We interact with people who tell us truths about the world we live in, based on what they have experienced, and we use our own ability of logic to experiment with induction and deduction to figure out what is true and what is not.

2: THE UNSEEN KNOWLEDGE

This is what I like to call light, and there is a type that is for everyone and a type exclusively for people chosen by Allah. This kind of knowledge is beyond all the information we can observe with our five senses. It is a guidance, and when I refer to "inspiration," I mean this unseen knowledge. This unseen knowledge which has reached every human being is either from within us or outside of us.

THE LIGHT WITHIN US

There is a depth within us all that is our most pure. It is like a light, a basis of right and wrong — our morality — and it gives us this inherent need for justice and compassion. It also recognizes that there is something greater than us, Allah, the One true God, with no partners. This origin of this light within us is when Allah took the souls of the children of Adam from his back, and we all testified to the oneness of Allah:

And remember when your Lord brought forth from the loins of the children of Adam their descendants and had them testify regarding themselves. Allah asked, 'Am I not your Lord?' They replied, 'Yes, You are! We testify.' He cautioned, 'Now you have no right to say on Judgment Day, 'We were not aware of this.' [2]

This testimony created an imprint upon us, our *fitra*, which is a state that we were born in, a guide for morality. It is our natural disposition and inclination toward good.

When we came into this world, this purity of truth was strong and untouched. However, as we grew, influences from outside us began to have an impact on our light. According to Ibn Taymiyyah, it was covered by biases, conjecture, ulterior motives, bad habits, blind following, and inherited beliefs,[3] and this covering of our light swayed our morality based on the norms of our parents or society at the time. This meant that it became harder for us to see the difference between right and wrong.

"Each child is born in a state of fitrah, but his parents make him a Jew or a Christian. It is like the way an animal gives birth to a normal offspring. Have you noticed any (young animal) born mutilated before you mutilate them?" [4]

THE LIGHT OUTSIDE OF US

Because this light within has been covered, Allah does not hold us accountable for the choices we made based only on it. Allah sent another light outside of us which was the revelation from Him to the prophets and messengers, who then came to show us truth and how to follow it. Their message was to remind us of who Allah is through His Lordship, singling Him out in worship and through His names and attributes:

WHO ALLAH IS THROUGH HIS LORDSHIP [5]

This means to single out Allah through His actions: He creates. Gives life. Takes life. Sustains life. All these acts are unique to Allah.

WHO ALLAH IS THROUGH
SINGLING HIM OUT IN WORSHIP [6]

This is the biggest reason the messengers and prophets came. Their message changed everything, starting from the very core of our being to every act we did. There was a kind freedom to being a slave to none other than the One worthy of our worship, however the people who didn't want to submit because of their own agendas resisted this the most.

WHO ALLAH IS THROUGH
HIS NAMES AND ATTRIBUTES [7]

When we know more about Allah and His names, our relationship becomes personal. We know He is kind and merciful because we have seen this amongst ourselves. However, the reality of Allah's kindness is beyond our scope of fully understanding. For example, we know that on Earth, there is only 1% of Allah's mercy, and He has 99% for Himself. Knowing how merciful a mother is to her child, the enormity of Allah's mercy, in comparison, is unfathomable.

The way we know these attributes of Allah is that we affirm what Allah affirmed for Himself and what our Messenger ﷺ spoke of. We know Allah is free of all deficiencies, shortcomings, and negative qualities.

LEVELS OF UNSEEN KNOWLEDGE

There are two levels of depth to this: the first level is for everyone, which we talked about above when we spoke about the light within us and the light outside of us, and the second level is for the chosen. This unseen knowledge for the chosen is a special gift given to a person who practices spiritual discipline/training known as *rayada,* and they do this *rayada* with an attentive heart. This is the kind of knowledge that will be a central theme of this book, and it is more commonly known as "inspiration."

When our eyes meet the light of knowledge, we experience certain effects, and these are like beacons within us that show us that the light is impacting us in a good way.

➤ THE BEACON OF ENERGY

If the knowledge we gain is making us lazy, or it doesn't affect us, then either the knowledge we have gained is impure, or we are.

➤ THE BEACON OF BEING SELF-LED

We often think that knowing more about Islam or Allah means more responsibility and accountability. Though that, like every worthy pursuit, is partly true, knowledge doesn't actually make life harder, but it does the opposite in opening a whole new world of ease. We are no longer left in the grey area of confusion. We have the tools to become self-led instead of blindly following others who may not always know better, but whose certainty makes them seem like an authority because our own uncertainty allows them to.

➤ THE BEACON OF INSIGHT

True knowledge has the greatest impact when it enters our heart. It also allows us to have insight[8], and the greatest insight is to think well of Allah[9]. Life is rarely easy, and the nature of our existence is that we are either in a state of hardship or ease. Without knowledge of Allah, we can fall into a well-intentioned trap of questioning Allah's actions because of our compassion for those in pain. However, as we learn more about the nature of this life and Allah Himself, something unexpected happens within us: we begin to understand the way reality truly is and we see deeper than the surface of this reality. We gain insight which, according to Ibnul Qayyim al Jawziyyah, is

"a light that is placed within someone's heart from Allah where they can recognize the truth that Allah sent His messengers."

AT A GLANCE

In this part, I will do a quick summary of all the need-to-know points, in case in the future you want to look back and remind yourself of the most important ideas:

Knowledge can be either what we perceive through our five senses, or from the unseen.

The unseen knowledge has one level which is for everyone to receive and another which is only for those chosen by Allah and it can be attainable though spiritual training. True knowledge gives us energy, helps us to be more self-led, and enters our heart, giving us insight.

A space for greatness

AISHA BINT ABU BAKR

Some of these concepts might be hard to put into context, so in some chapters, I'll use real-life examples of women who became exemplary in some aspect related to the content of the chapter.

For the chapter of knowledge, I want to give space to Aisha Bint Abu Bakr. She was a poet, a scholar, and one of the top narrators of hadith, narrating a monumental number of around 2,210 hadith. She also taught the Companions of our final Messenger ﷺ the religion. After he died, she continued to share the legacy of her beloved husband, our final Messenger ﷺ, and it was her lap that his head lay upon as he took his last breath and returned to Allah.

one small thing

I will be sharing these at the end of each chapter with small, achievable steps you can accomplish today.

Once a week, spend 30 minutes learning about Allah and Islam. In the Look Deeper section at the end of the book, I have listed some resources that you can begin with.

insights

CHAPTER 2

WISDOM

"Wisdom is doing what you need to do in the way you need to do it in the time you need to do it."

- Ibnul Qayyim al Jawziyyah

I once had a friend who wanted to learn more about Islam, so we went to a mosque. The first lady who spoke to her said, "You're going to have to start wearing a hijab." I looked over to my friend who suddenly became more self-conscious, touching her hair, and she looked back at me uncomfortably. Yes, in Islam, we women do wear hijabs. That knowledge was correct, but what was the issue here?

Wisdom in Arabic is *hikmah*, which means everything in its proper place. The sister's advice was given too soon, and what should have come first was an explanation of who Allah is, before insisting on His rulings.

Knowledge is a tool. It can be used to gain wisdom or to commit injustice, and we see this through how some of the most powerful and intelligent nations in the world are the most corrupt. There are four pillars upon which wisdom stands.[10] I want you to repeat them with me so you can implement them in your own life.

THE PILLAR OF KNOWLEDGE | ILM

Say it with me: I will learn and practice my knowledge.

We studied a whole chapter on knowledge, and wisdom begins with knowledge. The more knowledge we have, the greater our capacity for wisdom.

WISDOM IN ACTION

In this part, I will speak about a personal experience I had with wearing my hijab. When I was in high school, a boy took my hijab off in the busy halls after classes had finished. Everyone looked at me and laughed as I rushed away, quickly covering my head again to cope with the feeling of nakedness.

Later, I began to feel anxiety around hijab. I would see others wear it and feel distant from them. I ended up taking my own hijab off and I became antagonistic towards the hijab and those who wore it.

After I recommitted to Islam, I felt like a new Muslim, as if a veil had been lifted from my eyes. No matter how much I tried, I couldn't bring myself to even approach the idea of wearing my hijab, even though I felt like a part of me was missing without it. I was on edge whenever a covered Muslim woman walked past me on the street, and I would dread having to make conversation with Muslims in case they asked me why I didn't wear it.

With knowledge, the first pillar of wisdom, I could either choose to ignore the source of my feelings, the trauma associated with it, and push those emotions down, or I could question those feelings and learn the cause of my triggers.

THE PILLAR OF FORBEARANCE | HILM

Say it with me: I shall be forbearing with people.

The Arabic word for forbearance, *hilm*, is difficult to translate into

English. The closest word is "emotionality." It is the physical manifestation of our emotions, visible to those around us. When someone describes us women as "too emotional," it implies that emotions are a bad thing. But emotions are not bad; they are necessary for us to recognize our triggers, and when these emotions are extra strong, it is a signal that there might be an underlying issue, such as a trauma or a hormonal imbalance. The most important thing here is to be aware of our emotions so that we can work through them.

Wisdom is *not* to have a flatline of emotions, nor is it to have too many peaks. It is about being on the right wavelength. It is about the curves, not the spikes, and it is important to work towards smoothing our spikes.

> *Aslam al-Habashi reported: Umar ibn al-Khattab said, 'Let not your love be infatuation and let not your hatred be destruction.' It was said, 'How is this?' Umar said, 'When you love someone, you become infatuated like a child. When you hate someone, you love destruction for your companion.'*[11]

WISDOM IN ACTION

With my hijab experience, I could either give in to those intense emotions and react defensively if anyone questioned me about my lack of a headscarf, or I could try and process those feelings by writing in my journal or talking to someone I trust about them.

I could self-regulate by doing breathing exercises when things get intense. I could even do something as simple as drinking a glass of water or making *wudu* (ablution) like our Prophet ﷺ taught us in times of anger, which would help bring me back to my senses. And I know these techniques because I learned about them. I have *knowledge* about how to deal with my intense emotions.

JUSTICE | ADL[12]

Say it with me: I will know my biases and be just.

The opposite of *hikma* in Arabic is *dhulm* which means "something in the wrong place" and is more commonly translated as "injustice." When we are oppressive and transgressive, we act in the total opposite of wisdom.

WISDOM IN ACTION

With the story of my hijab, I could post a really mean tweet on how girls in hijabs should just take it off because it doesn't even look nice (bear with me please!), or I could know that my own biases are guiding my fingers on that mean tweet and be even nicer to my sister in hijab, maybe even a little curious.

DELIBERATION | ANAA

Say it with me: I will reflect upon the world around me and my actions.

With so much noise and clutter around us and within us, pausing and contemplating can be difficult but it is crucial to have a certain level of silence during our day. This silence will allow us to think before we react to a trigger which can be especially hard if that trigger is a person who is demanding a reaction immediately.

To deliberate is not a common practice amongst most of us, and when someone practices it, they might be labeled as unemotional, or passive-aggressive. However, the wisest of us think before we act or react, and the greatest way to bring true calm inside of us is through standing in the silence of the night and praying to Allah while the world sleeps.

WISDOM IN ACTION

With my hijab story, I could either bury my emotions, ignore them, and distract myself with the latest Netflix binge and a few hours of scrolling and hating on my hijabi sisters on Instagram and TikTok, or I could read that journal I wrote about my feelings around hijab. I could take a few moments to think gently about why I feel the way I do. I could take time away from social media and turn inward toward my feelings and be curious about the messages they are sending me.

In this next part, we will talk about where to find wisdom and the levels of it. It is also important to note that like knowledge, though there is a God-given level of wisdom, there is a lower level of it which we can work toward achieving through spiritual practice and study. With the following hierarchy, most people source their wisdom from the bottom up, meaning from the lowest hierarchy to the highest.

THE HIERARCHY OF WISDOM[13]

ALLAH

Allah is the ultimate source of wisdom, and He wants our humbleness. Have you ever seen an arrogant wise man? To begin our pursuit of wisdom, we must first become humble. When we turn to Him with the brokenness of humility which life inevitably throws to us, we will understand that Allah grants us favors that are truly in our best interest.

The unadulterated word of Allah is the Quran, and in reading His words and understanding them, we will grow in wisdom.

OUR FINAL MESSENGER MUHAMMED ﷺ

The story of the life of our final Messenger ﷺ is full of examples and inspiration. Here we learn true wisdom, and through the example of our final Messenger ﷺ we learn how to follow the Quran.

Qatadah reported: I said to Aishah , 'O mother of the believers, tell me about the character of the Messenger of Allah, peace and blessings be upon him.' Aisha said, 'Have you not read the Quran?' I said, 'O course.' Aisha said, 'Verily, the character of the Prophet of Allah ﷺ was the Quran.'[14]

THE BELIEVERS

The believers are our guides toward the highest source of wisdom, Allah, but they are not the ultimate source of wisdom. Not all believers are equal in belief and wisdom; however, it is among the believers that we will find the most wise of us, and they are the safest source of wisdom.

> *Abu Huraira reported: "The Messenger of Allah ﷺ said, 'The word of wisdom is the lost property of the believer. Wherever he finds it, he is most deserving of it.'"*[15]

There are different levels of wisdom among the believers, and above all are the scholars, who are the inheritors of the prophets in knowledge. The first followers of the Prophet ﷺ , the generation after him, and the generation after them are the known as the "pious predecessors." Abdullah ibn Mas'ud reported: The Prophet ﷺ said:

> *The best people are those of my generation, then those who come after them, then those who come after them. Then, there will come people after them whose testimony precedes their oaths, and their oaths precede their testimony.*[16]

HUMANITY

Only a person who is grounded with Quran and Sunnah can properly discern from the wisdom of anyone, regardless of faith and background. This is important because before seeing what the wisdom of others is, we must be grounded in our own religion.

Our Messenger ﷺ spoke about a wise man called Mut'im ibn 'Adi who was a non-Muslim and who had offered his protection to our Messenger ﷺ.

Years later, after the battle of Badr, Muslims had captured prisoners of war and our Messenger ﷺ said that if this man, Mut'im, were still alive and asked him to free those prisoners, he would have done so.[17]

LIVING CREATURES

When we observe our beautiful Earth, which is a living creature, and all the animals around us, there are so many lessons we can learn. Some of these lessons have been shared through the Quran itself, where two whole chapters are named after the bee and the ant, creatures of community, hard work, and healing the world.

There is a beautiful scene in the series "Our Planet" where a city called Chernobyl was declared as unlivable because of the high radiation from a nuclear explosion in 1986. The scene shows a building with leaves growing on it, and as the camera pans out, a magnificent display is revealed where a whole forest has grown over just a few decades in this city which was once full of people but is now reclaimed by Earth. Another testament of Earth's resilience in this example is how the predators who are the wolves have also returned, meaning that wildlife in the city which once fell from a radiation disaster is now thriving. Even after the biggest of disasters, our Earth still rises, and gives and grows. And of course, we are made from the soil of this Earth, and we are also connected to her.

THE UNIVERSE

In the secularized trend of society, when a person wants to attribute goodness from somewhere, they might say something like, "The Universe provides for me," or "The universe knows what's good for me." In the hierarchy of wisdom, the universe is but a sign of wisdom, not the source, and its place in the hierarchy is the lowest.

In the growing awareness of our natural inclination, our *fitra*, a movement toward becoming more mindful and turning inward is gaining momentum. With this new consciousness, people are understanding there is something greater than us. However, like in the past, today it is still being attributed to the creation, not the Creator, because the idea of God might be too distasteful. Instead, the words "source" or "universe" are used.

When I say the universe, I mean the cosmos, as in the science of how everything functions. But as I said, the creation, no matter how amazing, is only a sign of Allah's greatness and a means for our ultimate goal of worshipping Allah.

AT A GLANCE

Wisdom means "everything in its proper place."

It stands on the pillars of knowledge, forbearance, justice and deliberation.

The sources of wisdom are in this order: Allah, His Messenger ﷺ, the believers, humanity, living creatures, and the universe.

A space for greatness

KHADIJA BINT KHUWAYLID

Khadija was the first wife of our final Messenger ﷺ and she was wise in so many ways. One instance stands out to me where the Archangel Gabriel gave her the greeting of peace from Allah Himself, and her response was, "Allah is Peace (As-Salam), and from Him is all peace, and may peace be on Gabriel."[18] When I think about how she responded to hearing from Allah, the Creator of everything, I'm blown away by her wisdom.

one small thing

Designate a part of your day where you don't do anything except reflect. A super tip is to add *tahajjud*, the night prayer, to your schedule, even if you wake up just a few minutes before *fajr*.

insights

Chapter 3

SURRENDER

When we hear the word "surrender," we often think it means to give up, or to give our control away, but in Islam, it is a very intentional act. It is a state of being where we open ourselves to being guided in the right direction, on the path of our true purpose, our Big Why.

When we are in a state of true surrender, inspiration becomes clearer because the foundation of our self has been given strength through all we have learned in this book so far, and through the act of surrendering to the truth.

There are four principles to surrendering:

TO ALLAH WE BELONG
AND TO HIM WE WILL RETURN[19]

The first principle is to understand that we do not own anything, even ourselves. Our bodies are a gift, and it is important to treat them as we treat someone we love, like a mother to her child. If we were to over-indulge our child with sweet treats and salty snacks, we know that in the long run we are causing the child pain, even if in the moment they are happy (I fully support sweet treats. They make me happy, but I remind myself kindly to eat them in moderation).

Treating our bodies as if they belong to Allah also means mediating our inner talk so we can inspire and guide ourselves to do better, instead of shaming and self-criticizing.

Through this lens of understanding that we belong to Allah, our trials become easier to face because ultimately everything and everyone is here for the same reason, and in the end we will all go back to Allah, the One who created everything, the Most Just, the source of all good, and the Most Merciful — more merciful than our own mothers are to us.

This is freeing. There is a richness of not needing to attach to people or things in an unhealthy way, but rather surrendering from a place of wisdom, where everything is in its proper place, including the context of our Big Why, which is to worship Allah.

There is little room for arrogance in truly knowing Who gave us everything. Our grief becomes more bearable; though we still feel it, it enters a greater context of everything belonging to Allah.

RID THE MIND OF THE CLUTTER OF CONJECTURE AND LET IT BE FORMED BY THE REVELATION OF ALLAH

The things we watch and listen to affect how we act and what we write. Being real isn't always being real to the best part of us, and I will talk more about this in the chapter of the blinders in Part II.

There is an abundance of profanity, nudity, and inappropriate acts around us in the name of being "real," so much so that when we speak up against this, people might see us as strange, or label us as being "extra" or "extreme."

But when we listen to the unease of our heart upon hearing something which doesn't sit right with us, and we follow it, we will find something better. We will feel more wholesome and more authentic to our values, and this leads to our best self.

This unease in our hearts is like a contraction and feels like our chest is tight. It is the opposite of when we experience something good, and our hearts feel open and full.[20]

This voice of unease within us is made stronger through the purity of the word of Allah. When our minds are molded through revelation, the lens of how we see reality becomes polished and our hearts become soft. A soft heart means we are alive. We are present. What we do matters.

LET THE KNOWLEDGE OF REVELATION
ENTER THE HEART

We spoke about what true knowledge is supposed to do for us, and one of those things is to give us insight. It is very different to know something, and to feel it. The Companions of our final Messenger ﷺ would take years to finish memorizing just one chapter of the Quran because their focus went beyond learning to just know things. Their goal was to let Allah's words enter their hearts deeply, in a way where they fully immersed themselves, so every act from that knowledge was intentional. And that is why they were the greats; may Allah be pleased with them.

BE READY FOR WHATEVER PATH ALLAH SHOWS US

This can be scary. If you have lived your whole life in a certain way, and then new knowledge comes to you, it can be difficult to let go of what is familiar and embrace the unknown.

Our minds are wired to repeat patterns because in the past, this strategy helped us to survive. However, sometimes the patterns we are used to are no longer good for us, maybe even toxic, and that means it's time for a change, or time to let go. Fear of change can be our biggest barrier to growth, and that is something that we need to work on personally.

If you are confident that the change you are being guided to is guidance from Allah, and you find comfort in that, be ready to let go of that thing or things that are keeping you stuck or in a downward spiral. Embrace this new path of life, surrendering to it fully with love.

Surrendering in Islam is to understand that there is a greater wisdom than our own, and that all wisdom is from the ultimate source of wisdom, Allah.

We may not understand the details, how the carpet of the world we tread is but a thread in the bigger picture. The only One who sees everything is the Creator of it all, Allah. In the next chapter, we will talk about the decree of Allah and what true manifestation means to the Muslim.

AT A GLANCE

Surrender is intentional and active.

The four principles of surrender are: to acknowledge that we belong to Allah, to rid the mind of the clutter and let it be formed by the revelation of Allah, to let the knowledge of revelation enter the hearts, and to be ready for whatever path Allah shows us, even if it means everything changes.

A space for greatness

MARYAM BINT IMRAN

This space is for Maryam Bint Imran, the mother of Jesus. When the angel Gabriel approached her in the form of a man, she didn't know he was angel and told him to fear Allah, the Most Merciful. When she discovered her decree determined by Allah, she accepted it. In a community whose judgement would be overwhelming, she was going to be a mother to a son without a father. This was undoubtedly more daunting than the pain of giving birth. And yet, she surrendered to her decree. Most people in her position would have tried to defend themselves, but she obeyed Allah, who told her to remain silent.

Instead, her infant child spoke from the cradle, clearing her name and telling the people of his purpose, which was to be a messenger from Allah. And it all began with his mother, Maryam whom a whole chapter in the Quran is named after because she surrendered to a path Allah chose for her.

one small thing

Make time to read the Quran for ten more minutes than you do now, in whatever capacity you can. Set a timer, and during those ten extra minutes of Quran, focus on the meaning. Recite out loud in a slow, melodic voice for the full benefit, one of which is the stimulation of the vagus nerve, which helps our nervous system relax through lowering heart rate, reducing blood pressure, and calming the mind and the body.

insights

Chapter 4

MANIFESTATION

Have you ever heard someone say, "I manifested my destiny!" or "I manifested the love of my life!"? They are partly right in understanding that they have a will to allow things to happen, but the missing piece is that their will is bound to a greater will than their own. Before digging into this layered topic, let me clarify what I mean by manifestation. In Islam we call it *qadr* which means "decree" or "will." The two areas of *qadr* are from Allah and from humanity.

ALLAH'S MANIFESTING

The linguistic meaning of *qadr* is "to give something form or shape," such as Allah making the Earth in four days, but the meaning according to *shariah* goes much deeper. *Shariah* is the way we worship Allah through the guidance of His Messenger Muhammed ﷺ and the meanings of the Arabic words related to this are practical and apply to the context of Islam itself. *Qadr* is on four levels.

THE FIRST LEVEL:
ALLAH'S PRIOR KNOWLEDGE OF ALL THINGS | ILM

This means that Allah's knowledge is absolute; He knows what will happen, what has happened, what is happening, and the outcome of all the things which could have happened but didn't happen (I hope I didn't lose you). He knows everything and everyone including you and me and, in His knowledge, He is closer to us than our jugular vein.

You might have heard of "the butterfly effect"[21] where a flutter of a wing of something as small as a butterfly can be the cause of a disaster in some other part of the world. With this example in mind, Allah's knowledge encompasses the very smallest of details that many of us might not have even known existed, or at the very least, thought were insignificant.

"Not a leaf falls but He knows it..."

Quran[22]

When Allah removed the souls of humanity from the loins of our father Adam, He split these souls into two groups. One group was destined for hell and the other for heaven, *because* of this prior knowledge of Allah knowing everything.

"Allah took out all of Adam's offspring and made them testify to the oneness of Allah."

Quran[23]

THE SECOND LEVEL:
THE WRITING OF ALL OF THAT IS IN THE
PRESERVED TABLET | KITAAB

Before anything was created in relation to our own existence as humanity, Allah created the pen and He told it to write everything until the Day of Judgement in a book called the Preserved Tablet.[24]

"Do you not know that Allah fully knows whatever is in the heavens and the earth? Surely it is all written in a Record. That is certainly easy for Allah."

Quran[25]

The writings of the decree of Allah are of different types; some can be changed, and others cannot. This is important for you to know before we talk about our own power to bring our will to fruition.

The writings which cannot be changed are the ones where our destination of heaven or hell have been written, such as in the Preserved Tablet[26] and what was written when we were in our mother's womb.

Anas ibn Mālik reported that the Prophet ﷺ said: "Allah has appointed an angel in charge of the womb, and the angel says: 'O Lord, (it is) a sperm drop! O Lord, (it is now) a clot! O Lord, (it is now) a piece of flesh.' Then, when Allah wills to complete its creation, the angel asks: 'O Lord, (will it be) a male or female? Wretched (an evil doer) or blessed (doer of good)? How much will his provisions be? How long will he live?' All that is written while the fetus is still in his mother's womb."[27]

Some of the writings of the decree that can be changed, however, are the yearly writings which are determined on the Night of Decree[28], which falls on one of the last ten days of Ramadan, and there are more. So how can we influence the writings of our decrees which *can* be changed?

1. Asking Allah for anything we want, which is *dua*.

2. Keeping ties of kinship.

It was narrated that Anas ibn Maalik said: I heard the Messenger of Allah ﷺ say: "Whoever would like his rizq (provision) to be increased and his life to be extended, should uphold the ties of kinship."[29]

THE THIRD LEVEL:
ALLAH'S WILL | MASHEEAH

There are two parts to this:

➤ Allah's wish[30]: This is what Allah wants to happen. He always wants good for us and for us to be happy.

➤ Allah's will[31]: This is what actually does happen, and this might not always align with Allah's wish, but due to Allah's perfect knowledge, wisdom, and justice, it must come to be.

When someone chooses to worship Allah and they actually do it, Allah's will and wish align. But when a person does not, Allah's will and wish do not align because of the choice the person made. So, to be clear,

Allah is NOT pleased with everything He brings into existence.

THE FOURTH LEVEL:
ALLAH BRINGING THINGS INTO EXISTENCE | HALQ

Allah willed all that is, has been, and will be to occur on a set date and time. Even if the whole world tried to stop the decree of Allah from manifesting, they would never be able to.

"Allah is the Creator of all things, and He is the Maintainer of every-thing."

Quran[32]

HUMANITY MANIFESTING

Now that we have a basis of how manifestation comes into being from Allah, we can learn what our part is. We also have a will as humanity, but our will is within the will of Allah. For our will to come into being, to "manifest,"' there are three things we need:

➤ Allah allowing it to happen

➤ Our own willpower to do it

➤ The actual ability to carry it out

So, for example, if a person wants to get some milk from the fridge to make a hot chocolate with melted marshmallows, but they are too sick to leave their bed, they simply will not be able to make a delicious mug of hot chocolate.

As Muslims, we do not expect things to happen by just asking for them. There are actions that must follow, even if they are as small as picking up the phone and asking your mother to come over and bring some hot chocolate with marshmallows.

Yes, Allah created everything — including our actions — and a part of this is that we are the doers of them. There are inherent qualities within us that were put there by Allah, and we have the choice to act with the free will we have been given.

If everything is already willed, then what's the point?

Allah has prior knowledge of everything; hence it is written, but this does not mean we are forced to do anything. That is the whole point of our own free will, which really means the ability to choose.

Again, knowledge of Allah and thinking well of Him is important. One of Allah's names is the Most Just and another is the Most Wise. Though we have been given an initial programming of the soul, our *fitra*, we will never be judged only upon that inner guidance, *until the revelation comes to us*. This is from His justice.

However, when guidance has come, and the path to heaven has been made clear, it is from Allah's wisdom that when a person wants to be guided, Allah will make the path easy for them, knowing us more than we can ever know ourselves.

THE LAW OF ATTRACTION

The basic idea of this theory is that if you do good, then you get good, and likewise, if you do bad, then you get bad.

There are laws in the universe, and these are called "Allah's sunnah" which means Allah has a way. He created this world in such a way that what we put out will come back to us in a similar manner.

There are many examples of Allah's sunnah in both the Quran and Sunnah of His final messenger, such as if you call upon Allah, He will respond to you[33]. Another one is if you are grateful, Allah will give you more[34].

On a grander scale, another sunnah of Allah is that the truth will always be shown, even if falsehood seems to be everywhere.[35]

When people talk about the law of attraction, they have observed this pattern of like meeting like, and I call this "the Formula." The Formula is the way the world works— the system of the laws of the universe all around us—and through observation, some people have noticed it.

They have a deep knowledge of the Formula, but just like the statement "I manifested my own destiny" is incomplete, so is the Formula.

The point of all these signs around us — the like attracting like, and truth always overcoming falsehood, and being grateful giving us more

— is to turn to the One who created it all. The point of the Formula is to point us to Allah.

I know that this topic is a heavy one, so I wrote a poem which I hope can make things clearer.

Do not dwell on your prior destination of heaven of hell

Act

Determine which one you will achieve

Heaven will be made an ease

For some

And hell for others

And in all of this we

have a choice

AT A GLANCE

Allah has a will, and humanity have a will.

Humanity's will is bound to Allah's will.

Allah has a way, and one of the laws of this way is "like attracts like," and the point of that is to point to Allah.

A space for greatness

ASIYAH THE WIFE OF PHARAOH

In her final moments, after all the suffering her abusive and narcissistic husband had put her through, after all the emotional pain through the years, and having to hide her faith in Allah from him, Asiyah's end came violently and mercilessly from the people she had been surrounded by. And yet, she died smiling.

She knew that the true goodness of this world never lay in her beauty, even though she was the most beautiful woman anyone could imagine, nor was it in riches, even though her husband was the leader of Egypt. True goodness lay in ultimately being close to Allah, and the last thing she said before she died was:

> *"My Lord, build for me near You a house in Paradise and save me from Pharaoh and his deeds and save me from the wrongdoing people."*
>
> **Quran**[36]

The reason she died smiling is because Allah showed her that He answered her dua.

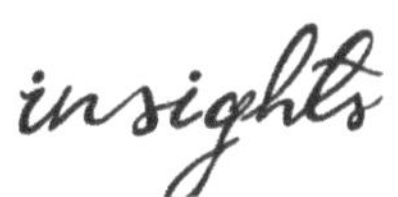

one small thing

Write a list of things you really want. Ask Allah for them and do one small thing in your power today to work toward getting your supplication answered.

I want to congratulate you on completing the first and most important part of this book. I know it's been intense. Thank you for sticking with me. Before we go to the next part, make sure you stretch your legs and maybe grab a mug of hot chocolate with marshmallows (or any beverage of your choice!) and when you're ready, let's dive in!

insights

Part II

THE EYE

This is the sight.

The nurturing that only a woman can clothe herself with

Falling in love with her reflection

As she raises her eyes to heaven

It is the reception of light.

The clarity earned by the wise

It is the work of the one whose heart is wide.

The cure to the disease

The cure to the dis-ease.

The pledge of the Woke,

it is to see.

To face.

To brace for the next part,

In the name of God.

CHAPTER 5

INSPIRATION | ILHAM

Part I was about setting the foundation of our ability to see the light of Allah's guidance. In this part we will talk about the way we see things, what kinds of light Allah sends to us, and how to recognize if the light is not entering our eyes due to blinders. As creatives, we are led by inspiration. In this chapter we will talk about inspiration itself and answer important questions like: *Are there different kinds of inspiration? When do we use it? What place does inspiration have in Islam?*

I will use the term *ilham* and inspiration synonymously, but the word *ilham,* like most Arabic words, covers a much wider scope than the direct English translation, "inspiration." It is crucial to know that inspiration itself can come from different sources, such as ourselves and the devil, which I will cover later in Part II. However, this chapter is dedicated to the inspiration from Allah only.

THE ISLAMIC STANCE ON INSPIRATION

The Islamic scholars differed in their stance on the significance of inspiration in our lives, and there are two main views on it, depending on the Islamic discipline of the scholar's focus. For example, the ones most opposed to it are those who talk of it from the aspect of law. The two main views on *ilham*:

IT HAS LITTLE VALUE.

The proof some scholars used was that Allah said in the Quran:

"And if you are in doubt about what We have sent down upon Our Ser-vant [Muhammad ﷺ], then produce a Surah the like thereof and call upon your witnesses other than Allah, if you should be truthful."

Quran[37]

If *ilham* can be a proof, then the challenge in the Quran would be nothing, hence *ilham* is not a proof of anything, and Islam is an evidence-based religion.

IT HAS GREAT VALUE.

"Oh, you who believe, if you fear Allah, He will give you a criterium for this Furqaan by which you distinguish right from wrong..."

Quran[38]

This verse means that Allah will teach us, and that teaching is more than the revelation of the Quran. Those whom Allah has not provided light, will not have light. The verse above is about the knowledge which is cast into the heart by Allah.

Another source that supports inspiration is:

And on the authority of Wabisah-Bin-Mabad who said: I came to the Messenger of Allah ﷺ and he ﷺ said, "You have come to ask about righteousness." I said, "Yes." He ﷺ said, "Consult your heart. Righteousness is that about which the soul feels at ease and the heart feels tranquil. And wrongdoing is that which wavers in the soul and causes uneasiness in the breast, even though people have repeatedly given their legal opinion [in its favor]."[39]

We spoke about the feeling of unease in the chapter of Surrender in Part I, and this is the hadith that describes that feeling more.

Each category above can go to extremes, with some completely disregarding the value of inspiration, and others putting inspiration in a place above revelation. For example, we have been asked by Allah to pray five times a day, so anyone who states that they have received an inspiration that tells them they do not have to pray has gone beyond the bounds of Islam.

As the people of the Quran and the Sunnah[40], we take the stance of moderation, a middle path. This means we believe inspiration has value, but only with the following bounds, which I placed at the beginning of this book for easy reference.

ONE | Any Woke hunch is inferior to the revelation of Allah in clarity, certainty, and proof value.

TWO | Our Woke hunches are uncertain and subjective. The testimony of the heart is not enough to be proof of anything.

THREE | Our Woke hunches are exclusive to us. They are not binding on others.

FOUR | Our Woke hunches have a limited scope: they have no place in religious rulings.

Now let's move on to the different types of inspiration which itself is a kind of guidance. When Allah sends us guidance, it is tailor-made for us and it is personal in a way which will affect us the most and help us to grow toward Him.

THE THREE LEVELS OF INSPIRATION

1. WAHY

Wahy is revelation, a special kind of inspiration only for messengers and prophets, and there is no room for error.

2. ILHAM | TAHDEETH

Ilham is the word for all the other kinds of inspiration, and it is a level below *wahy*. *Tahdeeth* is the strongest form of *ilham* and can be received by anyone other than a prophet or messenger. Unlike *wahy*, it has room for error.

Ibn Taymiyyah, a prolific writer and scholar born in 1263, said that the Companion of our final Messenger ﷺ, Umar ibn Al-Khattab, was upon the highest station in closeness to Allah, and though he would receive this kind of inspiration, he never claimed it, and there were many instances where he listened to the opinions of the other Companions with humbleness and an openness to learn. There were also times when he made mistakes, such as when he disagreed with his fellow Companion, Abu Bakr.

Ibn Taymiyyah said there were people who received this very high level of inspiration who were called *Muhadithoon*. This phenomenon was common before the coming of our final Messenger ﷺ because the *wahy* of the Quran had not yet come to clarify things.

However, when our final Messenger ﷺ came, he left a path so clear that we were not in need of guides after him.

3. OTHER KINDS OF ILHAM

The third level of the hierarchy of inspiration is not in order, and these concepts overlap, though there are subtle differences in their meaning.

Astuteness | Firasa This is the ability to tell people apart, where you can differentiate the interior from the exterior. For example, you might meet someone and know things about them which other people do not. Though there is a God-given level of *firasa*; however, there is also a lower level that some people naturally have because of the way their minds are wired. Because this one is quite fas-

(CONTINUED ON PAGE 61)

(CONTINUED FROM PAGE 60)

cinating, the following two chapters will be covering it in more detail.

Audition | Ismaa This is where you can hear or see things that are lessons from Allah. For example, you might have a question about something and you read the Quran, and the verse is directly related to that question you had.

Understanding | Ifham The scholar whom some call the "doctor of the heart," *Ibnul Qayyim al Jawziyyah,* a student of Ibn Taymiyyah believed this was the highest level of inspiration within its class.

Disclosure | Kashf This is when something is hidden from others and Allah makes it clear to you.

Clarification | Bayaan This is where a clearness is achieved, and it can come in many forms, such as eloquent speech or seeing things more clearly.

Opening | Fath This is where something was very difficult but is then made easy. So, for example, you have been trying to finish writing your book for many years, but something keeps popping up which feels like a block. It might be your own inability to finish your book, or the difficulty of finding a decent editor, etc., but then something shifts, and suddenly you have this vigor and you're meeting people who can help you finish your book.

Taste | Dawk This literally means taste, but loosely translated it is what many might recognize as intuition. A person with *dawk* has the right sense about different things.

Nightly dream | Ruyaa Ibn ʿAbbās reported:

(CONTINUED ON PAGE 62)

(CONTINUED FROM PAGE 61)

The Messenger of Allah ﷺ said: 'O people, there is nothing remaining of the glad tidings of prophet-hood except a good vision that a Muslim sees or someone else sees it for him...'[41]

In Islam we can have different types of dreams. Good visions or dreams that bring us closer to Him are from Allah. Dreams that cause us anxiety and fear for no other reason but to hurt us are from the devil. Then there are dreams which are the chattering of the self that help us process the daily events through the dream state.

Criterion | Furqaan This is the ability to differentiate between misguidance and truth to refute misconceptions.

WHERE DO WE USE INSPIRATION?

There are four main places where we might use inspiration.

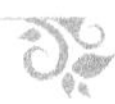

➤ *Things which are generally permissible:* So, for example, if two marriage proposals came to you, something might be cast in your heart that guides you to the right potential spouse.

➤ *Religious matters:* Our scholars of Islam are like lamps that make guidance clear to us. However, there might be issues that have been disputed, so the answer to a question is not clear. In these times, it is important to consult our hearts when something is unclear. This extra guidance, this inspiration from Allah, will aid us in times of ambiguity.

➤ *Room in understanding:* When something happens to

(CONTINUED ON PAGE 63)

(CONTINUED FROM PAGE 62)

others, we ourselves can reflect on it, and likewise when something happens to us, others can reflect on it.

➤ ***Ilham helps us to find relief:*** You might have felt a great pressure or worry about something, and then Allah shows you something which brings you great ease.

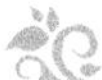

DO WE BELIEVE IN GOOD OMENS?

In a world where people have so many superstitions, we can find ourselves wondering if the black cat under a ladder was a sign that something bad was going to happen, or a broken mirror means danger — or whatever the common lore is about bad omens.

In Islam we believe in good omens, good signs such as synchronicities, good names, and so on. However, we do not believe in bad omens. Islam is a religion of optimism, and when we see good signs, this increases our good thoughts of Allah.

The Prophet ﷺ would seek good omens and not evil ones and he would become pleased by a good name.[42]

INSPIRED BY ANGELS

An indirect way we are inspired by Allah is through His angels. Angels are heavenly beings made of pure light. They are part of the unseen world, and their only purpose is to worship Allah. The angels carry out duties for Allah including governing the physical world, managing the rain and weather, assisting us in our own purpose through writing our good and bad deeds, and inspiring us.

They do this through calling us only to good, and the more we adhere to a life of being Woke, the more they become attracted to us and remind us of positive thoughts.

As you can see, the topic of inspiration from Allah has many parts to it, but the main things to remember are the Bounds of the Woke and that inspiration comes in different forms, unique to us, but all as a loving guidance from Allah.

AT A GLANCE

Islam has a place for inspiration, but with bounds.

There are different kinds of inspiration.

Wahy is the highest kind of inspiration and has no room for error; all other kinds have room for error.

A space for greatness

THE MOTHER OF MOSES

Sometimes our circumstances feel impossible, but Allah inspires us in the most unimaginable ways. We can see this in the story of the mother of Moses, who had to make one of the most difficult choices a mother can, to separate from her child. She not only had to send her son away, but was instructed to put him in a basket and set him afloat in a river, because of all places, he would be safer there than in the hands of the tyrant Pharaoh.

When her heart began to waver with the overwhelming emotion of a mother separating from her infant child, Allah sent her inspiration in the form of peace in her heart. It was a feeling that everything would be ok, even though at that moment, she had no way of knowing how. Soon after, she was feeding her own milk to her son, who had ended up in the hands of Pharaoh as a kind of adoptee.

one small thing

Have you ever experienced any forms of the inspiration we spoke about? Maybe it was a dream you had which came true? Or you were thinking of something, and it happened. Maybe you experienced synchronicities? Write about this time. It can be a poem or a paragraph — there's no structure here, just reflection.

insights

Chapter 6

MENTAL ASTUTENESS[43]

There are two types of *firasa*, one mental, and the other spiritual. In this chapter, we will talk about mental astuteness from the perceptive of how the different parts of our brains work, how hormones can affect how we perceive people and the world, and how we can use wisdom to help us to grow in our mental astuteness.

Mental astuteness[44] is a kind of cleverness with people — being people smart — and it is not exclusive to the righteous. For example, Hitler was known for using this skill to sway crowds in his favor. Like knowledge, the skill of mental astuteness can be a gift for the righteous or a weapon for the corrupt.

Our brains are wired in a way that is formed through both our experience and our DNA, and wiring differs from person to person. We all have a unique perspective of the world, and this includes our capacity to understand people. Some individuals, like the fictional character Sherlock Holmes, created by Sir Arthur Conan Doyle, understand people through simply observing clues about them: the way they dress, the way they walk, and so on. Others might understand people through reading their emotions and in some capacity, being affected by them. Emotional Contagion is a theory that suggests that we begin to act or feel the way someone or others are feeling. The people we are surrounded by have an effect on us, the same way a good or a bad smell sticks to our clothes.

Many times, a person who has the deepest understanding of people in this emotional way is someone who has experienced the most difficult emotions through trauma. Some of the greatest healers in the world used to be children who experienced the greatest pain, such as the loss of a parent at a young age, or abuse.

THE RIGHT BRAIN AND THE LEFT BRAIN

Self-awareness is our biggest tool for mental astuteness. A part of this is understanding the two different parts of our brain: the right brain and the left brain. Both parts are significant, and it is important to have a balance. The right brain is the part that picks up on the feelings of other people, and the left brain is more attuned to details, like how they dress, for example.

Each part is unique, and both are useful and crucial for living our best lives.

THE LEFT BRAIN

This is commonly understood as "masculine energy,"; however, due to the connotations attached to this term such as "divine masculine," I have decided to steer clear of this wording.

When we are using the left brain, we are in a state of control, which is why we are more focused on giving to people, rather than receiving. Our rational thinking is dominant, and our core focus is to achieve goals. The world is split into smaller and identifiable parts, and our thinking is very linear. This part of our brain is about distinction and knowing *how* things work, rather than *why*.

It is not inherently a negative state to be in, but without balance, we can become overly controlling and narcissistic.

AN UNBALANCED LEFT BRAIN

Becoming very critical of everything: *"Ok so what if they created a masterpiece? Why didn't they create two?"*

Being controlling: *"Stand over here, not there. Right here in this square."*

Being overly competitive: *"Well, I did it first!"*

Being very reactive and always needing to be right: *"Let's solve this issue right away. I'm right and you're wrong."*

Other ways an unbalanced left brain can manifest is in being aggressive, being terrified of failure, being out of touch with the body, having overly-rigid boundaries, blaming others, and being withdrawn.

When our left brain is in balance, it serves as a wonderful problem-solving tool where a person is detail-oriented, which is intellect-based.

THE RIGHT BRAIN

This is commonly understood as "feminine energy" and again, due to what is implied by it such as "feminine divine," I have decided to use the term "the right brain." This is a state of surrender and what many of us would commonly understand as intuitive- based. A person using their right brain is very aware of the feelings in their body and are guided to understand the world and other people through this. They are more receiving and reflect more. They see the whole picture, rather than the parts, and everything is about being connected to each other and the self.

Using our right brain, we discover the *what* instead of the *how*, and we are more creative. Our connection to people is a deeper one that goes beyond words.

AN UNBALANCED RIGHT BRAIN

Becoming overly attached to things and people: *"I hate you... but I love you. Too much."*

Wanting to be saved: *"Well it happened to Cinderella, ok?"*

Having weak boundaries: *"Sure, I'll clean your house and mow your yard while you go on a trip to the Bahamas, even though I have a newborn baby."*

Some other ways the unbalanced right brain can manifest is having low self-worth, abandoning the self, being afraid to speak your truth, chasing love to feel valued, becoming manipulative, and having a victim mentality.

MENTAL ASTUTENESS
AND OUR WOMANLY FLOW

I would never have thought that our own womanly cycles would influence how our minds understand people, but they do! Our bodies are balanced by our hormones, and the quantity of hormones differ throughout our womanly cycles.

Every month, a woman who isn't pregnant, or just had a baby, or is in menopause should go through four phases where the hormones in her body affect how her body feels and thinks. It is important that we listen to our bodies when they feel a certain way. When we honor our bodies and their needs, we fall into a state of natural flow, as Allah created us, without fighting our beautiful nature. I don't want to bombard you with a whole lot of science, but if you want to look deeper, there are some amazing resources at the back of this book. For now, it is good to know that the hormones in our bodies do different things and these cause us to feel differently throughout our cycles. Estrogen is the nurturing hormone which gives us energy. Progesterone is the hormone that prepares us to give birth and it helps heighten our mood. Testosterone, usually associated with men, helps us with libido.

The cycle phases below are in averages in the number of days and can vary from woman to woman.

PHASE 1: MENSTRUATION, 3–7 DAYS
SUPERPOWER: REFLECTION

This is the time when the two sides of our mind have the greatest communication. We are simultaneously using the left brain and the right brain, and both sides are especially connected because our hormones, estrogen and progesterone, are at their lowest. We are most "intuitive" during this phase. This is a really good time to put the world on pause for a minute and turn inward.

It might not be the best time to be around people for too long because your energy is so low. Instead, this is the time to deliberate (the fourth pillar of wisdom) and decide if a choice in your life is working for you. Ask yourself things like, *How do I feel about that writing project?* or, *What was the problem in that relationship?*

Because our bodies are going to be tired, especially at the beginning of the cycle, it's ok to slow down our exercise routines and even take a nap or two.

PHASE 2: FOLLICULAR PHASE, 7–10 DAYS
SUPERPOWER: CREATIVITY

Personally, this is my favorite time of the cycle. We are more in the right brain, which means our mind is more open to experiencing new things and meeting new people. The ideas flow gorgeously, and as estrogen is rising, our mood is getting better, which affects how we see people and the world.

We can step into unknown territory here with more confidence. This is a good time to meet new people because we are armed with curiosity and a better mood, which help us to better manage our emotions and put our biases aside.

PHASE 3: OVULATION, 2-4 DAYS
SUPERPOWER: MAGNETIC

While ovulating, our communication with people is much deeper, and we can say what we mean more eloquently. Estrogen rises and so does testosterone, and this is a good time to have those heavy conversations with people.

Again, we are more in the right brain, and it is all about collaboration and teamwork.

PHASE 4: LUTEAL, 10-14 DAYS
SUPERPOWER: TASK ORIENTED

There is great wisdom in why this last part of our cycle is also the longest. The first three parts encourage us to put everything in its proper place, and in this final part, we now act upon it.

There are two parts to the luteal phase. At the beginning, straight after ovulation, our hormones progesterone and testosterone are at their peak, and we have more energy, but toward the end they lower, which means we have less energy.

There are also some days where the hormones are at a level that increases emotional intelligence, which uses parts of the right brain.

Towards the end of the phase, we move more into the left brain, where we might feel sad, and when we are sad, we notice details. We can utilize this as a strength by understanding that instead of overthinking why a person might have triggered us, we can hone the skill of observation by using it to strengthen what we are doing during this cycle phase.

A beautiful time to reflect is during the night prayer, especially if you're a mama and that's the only quiet you can get.

Over time you will observe your creative flow is unique to you, and the more attuned you are to being spiritually Woke, the more you will recognize your body and its flow. As I said, being Woke is a holistic approach, and everything feeds into everything else.

The key to all these phases is to be gentle with ourselves. These are all gifts, and ultimately, we belong to Allah, so it is important we honor the gifts He gives us.

LEVELING UP IN OUR MENTAL ASTUTENESS

It is amazing how wisdom can be practiced in so many ways. One of the most difficult things for us to deal with is other people, and yet they can also be the most fulfilling part of our lives. We will use the four pillars of wisdom which we covered in the chapter of wisdom to help us with this:

KNOWLEDGE: I WILL LEARN ABOUT MYSELF AND OTHER PEOPLE

We can do this through recognizing our own qualities, what triggers us, and what makes us feel happy or sad, and investigate these feelings. We can also take personality tests, which are a nice and quick way of learning about ourselves. However, I would say be careful of defining yourself only through them; their purpose is to help us go beyond what we think we are and work toward being better. You can learn about others through observing their behavior and how it affects you. Every trigger is a message, and in working through our triggers, we will naturally understand others, too. In understanding people, we can empathize with them (plus, write some phenomenal characters in our own stories!)

We can also observe our own cycles and how they affect our insights and lives.

FORBEARANCE: I WILL WORK ON BALANCING MY EMOTIONS

When we recognize our own emotions and where they are rooted, this self-awareness gives us clues to what we can focus and work on. As we said before in the chapter of wisdom, if our emotions are at peaks, there might be deeper issues that we should work on. For issues that overwhelm us or make everyday life too difficult, it can be useful to speak with a mental health professional.

JUSTICE: I WILL RECOGNIZE MY BIASES

We see our world through the lens of our experience, and we might not always be on the side of truth. For example, if someone was betrayed, and that betrayal trauma was not resolved through processing the experience fully, that person will have a difficult time trusting other people, no matter how genuine or kind they are.

It is important to honor our experiences and to recognize when a bad experience has affected us. However, we must not let our own bad experiences lead us to treating others unjustly. It is understandable when a person hurts someone because they have been hurt; however, in my opinion, there is never a valid excuse to hurt anyone, no matter how much pain you have been through.

DELIBERATION: I WILL DELIBERATE
BEFORE I REACT

To understand people emotionally and mentally is an amazing thing, but we must be careful not to assume things about the signals we receive. For example, when someone seems like they are in a bad mood, or in a rush to leave, it doesn't always mean they want to get away from us.

We will never know the real reason why people do things, and many times, behavior itself is subconscious, meaning the person who is doing it might not even be aware of their own actions. Trying to put a story together about a person based on things we observe from our mental astuteness can be biased, and only Allah knows what the full and true story is.

AT A GLANCE

The greatest way we can strengthen our understanding of people is self-awareness.

one small thing

Buy or make a diary for the year. It should be so beautiful that when you look at it, you feel warm and fuzzy. I want you to schedule your work and activities based on your cycle. You can find what day of cycle you are on through different phone apps which are inexpensive at your app store.

If you are a planner, like me, to work with your body as well as your mind might be hard at first, but over time, when you plan your weeks based on the state of both your body and mind, you will begin to find that things fall into place, God willing.

insights

CHAPTER 7

SPIRITUAL ASTUTENESS

We pride ourselves as a society on having greatly advanced in the realm of science and technology, but many of the things we do as humans have been consistent for thousands of years. When the Quran was revealed, it was a timeless guidance for all humanity, a witness to human nature, a message recognizing the patterns we fall into as our actions repeat from generation to generation, time and time again.

Two things that have been around as long as rational thought was recorded are the fortune teller and the astrologer. In stories, the name for this archetypal character is "the Seer," and these characters go back as far as Greek mythology, such as the Oracle of Delphi. Religions have been based on these "seers," and today, our movies and literature are still flooded with this concept which permeates giants like Disney, in movies such as *Aladdin and the King of Thieves* and *Hercules*. For me, living in New York, it feels like every lamppost or subway train has a flyer encouraging me to have my palm read and fortune told with promises of insight and healing.

In the chapter of inspiration, we spoke of some important boundaries when it comes to receiving inspiration from Allah, and I briefly mentioned how inspiration can come from other sources. In this chapter, we will speak about some of these sources which include where fortune tellers receive their knowledge, and we will also discuss what true spiritual astuteness is and some guidelines for it.

To reiterate the previous chapters, we as Muslims do believe in a kind of inspiration where a person knows things about people.

The Messenger of Allah ﷺ said:

"Beware of the believer's intuition, for indeed he sees with Allah's Light." Then he recited: "Surely in this are signs for those who discern."[45]

Quran[46]

Ibnul Qayyim al Jawziyyah further clarified:

"It is a light that Allah bestows in the heart of his servant, by which he distinguishes between truth and falsehood, advantage and disadvantage, the honest and the liar."

Spiritual astuteness is about interpreting subtle signs. It is a gift from Allah which is given to those who spiritually strengthen themselves, and a level of it can be given to both Muslims and non-Muslims who practice endurance and reflection. It is a guidance meant to bring us to Allah. There are different levels of spiritual astuteness, and to find out more information, there are resources in the back. For now, I will mention two.

➤ *A good shot by a bad shooter:* This means the knowledge can come from someone who is totally insignificant. You might not expect it from them because they don't have good character. The reason the unseen can be told to us by those without ranking with Allah is for the need of a sincere seeker to hear it.

As we mentioned, wisdom can still be harvested from the uncultivated hearts, and when we find wisdom in anything, we accept it as a good omen and nothing more. This is because without proper interpretation, we — unlike the scholars — could arrive at wrong answers.

➤ *The fruit of faith:* This type of spiritual astuteness is from the cultivated hearts, and it is the result of faith and the refinement of it through spiritual discipline[47]. This includes our compassion and good character toward people as well as controlling our doubts and desires by following the way of Allah and His Messenger ﷺ. When someone is given this level of spiritual astuteness, it is an honor from Allah to them.

Here are two keys to help us understand.

THE KEYS OF THE UNSEEN BELONG TO ALLAH

The unseen knowledge we receive from Allah is what He chooses to show us. The most well-known and the best of humanity who were given this gift were Allah's prophets and messengers. Allah chose to give them this knowledge.

Only the prophets and messengers would receive something called *mujizah*, which were miracles from Allah, such as the act of Moses splitting the sea by the permission of Allah, and Jesus healing the leper by the permission of Allah.

However, there are also miracles given to those whom Allah has chosen, and these are called *karamat*. Here is an example of that with Umar.

Naafi' said that 'Umar sent out a military detachment and he appointed a man called Saariyah in charge of them. Whilst 'Umar was delivering the khutbah one Friday, he said, 'O Saariyah, the mountain! O Saariyah, the mountain!' And they found out that Saariyah had moved towards the mountain at that moment on the Friday even though there was the distance of a month's journey between them.[48]

THE KEY IN OUR HAND CAN BE A MEANS
TO OPEN THE DOOR TO GOOD OR BAD

Spiritual astuteness is a gift, and it must be used wisely. The people who receive these gifts are chosen by Allah and they do not control them. The best way to know if a person is truly close to Allah[49] is what they use these gifts for, and depending on this, their gifts can either be a testimony of good or bad for them on the Day of Judgment.

The people who claim these gifts and use them to earn money are not what they say they are, and their sources of information are either themselves or the *jinn*[50]. When the Quran came as revelation, the angels were put as guards in heaven, and the devils could no longer hear the prophecy spoken by the angels.

The Prophet ﷺ said:

They (the jinn) would pass the information back down until it reaches the lips of a magician fortune-teller. Sometimes a meteor would overtake them before they could pass it on. If they passed it on before being struck, they would add to it a hundred lies.[51]

This means that if we truly receive the inspiration of spiritual astuteness, we cannot use this gift to show off or to manipulate others for personal gain. If a person does this, it is a sign they are not trustworthy.

So why were prophets able to show people their miracles?

Our prophets and Messenger ﷺ did not come to show off, but to show humanity the way of Allah. The miracles they received, the *mujizah*, were a means of doing this, and they helped strengthen the people's belief in their message.

However, when people show their miracles — their *kiramat* — intentionally, it can lead to blind following, and we see this in the numerous cults and leaders who have claimed divine knowledge. Most of the time, we will rarely know the righteous unless Allah chooses to reveal them to us because these special ones keep their relationship with Allah and the fruits of it guarded between them and Allah.

When we share the divine inspiration Allah gives to us, we are in danger of calling to the self, and this is dangerously opposed to the purpose of these gifts, which is to call to Allah. And remember, we can never be totally sure about any inspiration, unless it is revelation,[52] and the revelation was complete with the coming of our final Messenger Muhammed ﷺ. A poet said:

"If you see a man flying through the air or walking on the water, but he does not adhere to the limits of shariah, then you should realize that this is a temptation which is leading him astray, and he is a man of Biddah."[53] [54]

When I first learned about spiritual astuteness, there was great ease in knowing that everything we need has already been given to us by Allah, and when things become unclear, we have important guidelines which can bring us back to our Big Why. Our Big Why is to worship Allah, and this is our context of truly seeing the world, despite popular culture and what have become familiar story tropes of corrupt oracles with half-truths.

Sometimes the full truth is more elusive than we are used to because the ones who receive it from Allah use it to benefit humanity in a more subtle and wise way, using their gifts to call to Allah and not themselves. These are the unsung heroes, some of whom shake the hands of angels on the Night of Decree and whom most of us might never know.

AT A GLANCE

Allah knows the unseen without being told about it and He chooses whom He gives the knowledge of the unseen to.

Inspiration can be a good shot by a bad shooter, or from the fruit of faith.

There are limits to our gifts, and we should use them wisely.

A space for greatness

THE WIFE OF MOSES

When the wife of Moses first met him, she knew there was something special about him. She told her father to hire him because he was strong and trustworthy. We rarely hear her story, but there was something special about her too. She had a way of knowing that Moses was a good man, even though she had just met him. After telling her father about him, she married him and supported him in his journey to become a prophet and leader of one of the biggest nations in history.

one small thing

I want you to start observing the world around you and the people who claim to know things that others do not. Apply the lessons we have learned in how you observe them and also approach literature, movies, and so on with this new internal boundary.

insights

CHAPTER 8

THE STATE OF ABUNDANCE

We all want to be happy. For me happiness is to feel the joy of a cool breeze on a sunny day, the sound of the rain as it hits the pavement outside my window, the scent of a brand-new book as I breathe in the freshly-printed paper smell.

Quite often, we equate happiness with gratitude, but although being happy can lead to being grateful, it is much more likely that being grateful will lead us toward happiness[55].

Gratitude is a powerful gift, and while there is a part which comes from us, there is another which is given to us by Allah. The Arabic word for gratitude is *shukr* and it encompasses every part of us: our tongues, limbs and hearts. It is one of the biggest components of our faith and without it, we miss a chunk of our Big Why.

There are key points to remember about gratitude:

POINT ONE: GRATITUDE IS A STATE

It is a positive perspective on life, and through this lens, we recognize the best in any given situation.

POINT TWO: THE OPPOSITE OF GRATITUDE IS DISBELIEF IN ALLAH

When the devil[56] was expelled from Heaven, he promised Allah:

"I will approach them from their front, their back, their right, their left, and then You will find most of them ungrateful."

Quran[57]

The Arabic word for ingratitude is kufr which means to bury a seed. In the context of faith, kufr means to bury belief, and the most ungrateful ones are the ones who, like the devil, are the closest to arrogance. Have you ever met a grateful and arrogant person? Ingratitude is when one denies the favors of Allah which ultimately leads one to denying Allah Himself.

POINT THREE: GRATITUDE INVITES ABUNDANCE

Allah's law is: the more grateful we are, the more Allah gives to us, whether we are Muslim or non-Muslim. However, there is a higher level of gratitude which is only obtained by the believers, and this is because of point four.

POINT FOUR: ONLY THE BELIEVERS CAN GRASP THE TRUE MEANING OF GRATITUDE

Gratitude is what our belief in Allah should lead to, and the greatest show of gratitude is to follow Allah and His final Messenger ﷺ . We do this through:

➤ **Loving Allah by submitting to Him:** Love is an action which must be maintained, and our religion is headed by love.

Ibnul Qayyim al Jawziyyah said, "The heart on its path to Allah the Almighty is like a bird, where love is its head, and fear and hope are its wings."

To grow in our love for Allah, we must first know Allah through His revelation, the Quran. We then obey Allah through what He loves, which are the obligatory acts of worship: the five pillars of Islam[58]. Once we do these foundational acts, we can then grow our love for Allah through voluntary acts.

Abu Hurayrah narrated that our final Messenger ﷺ said:

Allah said: "... My servant does not come near to Me with anything more loved by Me than the religious duties I have enjoined upon him, and My servant continues to draw near to Me with supererogatory works so that I shall love him." [59]

➤ *Praising Allah for our gifts:* Allah gave us these personalized and unique gifts for a reason.

In a world of quick likes and follows, it is easy to think that sharing our gifts with the world is the focus. However, the more stimulation and satisfaction we seek, the less grateful we become for the smaller things.

Every skill we have been given, the place we live, and every part of us, down to the very nuances of our personality, are not a coincidence. Allah planned it to the very detail with precision, wisdom, and justice, as we learned in the chapter of Manifestation. Everything that Allah has given us is to help us live our Big Why. It is to remember Him and thank Him by using these gifts to please Him.

With all gifts, like all flaws, we have a choice on how we use them. A knife can be used to stab, or to cut bread for the hungry. A voice can be used to sell music albums, or to recite the Quran and to call to Allah. A word can be used to make peace or create war. We can use our gifts to help us in our greatest rise, or our greatest fall. With choice comes responsibility, and this is the essence of what it means to be a leader. The best leaders are the ones who lead the self.

THE CONNECTION OF PATIENCE AND GRATITUDE

In life, we are always between the bounty of Allah in times of ease and His justice in times of hardship.

A person who has reached excellence in faith will see both hardships and ease as one. But most of us must train ourselves to receive the decree of Allah — whatever it is — from a place of trust, patience, and gratitude, and this isn't always easy.

Both hardship and ease require patience or gratitude and sometimes both. However, the hardship we experience gives us a greater chance to reach true excellence in faith and to rise in our status with Allah. Our virtues are revealed through our reactions to hardship and ease, and it is these virtues that distinguish us. When we are patient during hard times, this shows the greatest virtues our species can have, such as for-bearance, kindness, courage, and so on.

To be in a state of abundance is a wonderful gift, and to practice it brings a long-lasting and fulfilling joy. A person might not be naturally grateful, but she can learn to be if she catches her thoughts and nurtures them into seeing the good side of things, beginning with something as small as the taste of that first cup of coffee in the morning. In the grand scheme of things, a coffee might seem insignificant, but what seems insignificant is quite often the pebbles which build mountains. Every good thing, every act of thanks to Allah, will bring the fruit of something greater.

It is also worth mentioning that though being in a state of abundance is when we are grateful, the most grateful acts are not for an agenda to gain abundance. They are because we recognize that life is beautiful, that we are beautiful, and that Allah is the Most Beautiful. And all praise to Allah[60] for everything.

AT A GLANCE

Gratitude is a state that invites abundance.

The greatest show of love is to obey Allah.

To greatest show of gratitude for our gifts is to use them to live our Big Why.

one small thing

Today I want you to use one of your gifts to help someone else. It could be that you see someone sad, and you write a poem to lift them up.

Or you have a beautiful smile, and you make a little child extra happy by smiling at them.

insights

CHAPTER 9

BLINDERS

Sometimes it is hard to see things clearly. We can do all the work to train our eyes, but there are still some things that will control our vision. These things will consume our thoughts, our bodies, and our hearts, so much that we become blind to the truth, and when inspiration comes from Allah, we misinterpret it or disregard it entirely because our sight is unable to accept it.

To do the work of the Woke Woman, we must first traverse the path of self-reflection. We must look into the mirror, shine the light of all we have learned and be honest in what reflects. In this chapter, we will talk about the various influences around us and within us that are tainting our eyes. If left unrendered, they will continue to do so, until we become completely blind to the light.

THE WOUNDED SELF

A wound is a hole which leaves us in parts. According to some definitions of trauma, when we have experienced something traumatic, we are left wounded, and this leads us to become fragmented and disconnected to the self. Every person has been wounded in some way, and this trauma overwhelmed their senses. If that trauma is unprocessed, it lives in our system and we become more susceptible to stressors, living in a way that is disconnected to the self. Some people have been through serious religious trauma, and so the idea of believing in an organized religion becomes difficult to them. Trauma is one of the greatest blinders we can have to being Woke.

When I first consciously came to Islam, I experienced a great peace, and it felt like the world finally made sense. After a few years, when the feeling became more distant, parts of me began to unravel, and I found that these unhealed parts were damaging to myself and to those around me. They became toxic blocks in my life, and I felt like I was losing my-self all over again.

It was through my research into this book, a few years back, that I heard about trauma and how it shows up in our lives. The idea struck me because I had never really thought of myself as traumatized. Yes, I'd had some difficult experiences, but how could they, all the way back then, make me feel like this, right now? So empty, stuck, and unmotivat-ed. So angry at the world and so sad deep down inside?

When we take the step toward healing, we are doing an important thing for ourselves and our loved ones. Healing comes in layers, and we are always in need of healing. If you think you may have some un-processed trauma, I advise you to speak to a mental health professional whom you trust to help guide you through the healing process.

THE MEAN VOICE IN OUR HEAD

As we traverse this path of Wokeness and come closer to our Small Why and Big Why merging as one gorgeous spectacle, we will find that the mean voices in our head might become louder and more chaotic. This mean voice can either be directed toward us or toward other peo-ple, and it can either be from parts of our own self, or from *Shaytan*[61].

When I speak about the mean voice, I don't mean the ones that are overwhelming; in that case, again I would advise you to speak to a men-tal health professional. In the general case of the mean voice, some of the things we hear ourselves think can be scary and make us feel like we are bad people, but there is a wisdom in that Allah does not hold us accountable for our thoughts. However, if we allow these negative thoughts to control us, they will become actions, subconsciously or consciously.

The thoughts that come from us might have been instilled in us when we were children and we received a lot of criticism. Most of the time these thoughts are trying to protect us — even the ones that say we are overweight or worthless. It can be hard to overcome those parts of us, and the key here is to separate ourselves from that mean voice and understand that those thoughts are not us — they are just part of us. These protective parts of ourselves can change how they show up in our lives through how we talk to ourselves. A kind word of support to ourselves can be a step toward helping us overcome our inner critic. At first, when we begin changing how we talk to ourselves, it can feel false or strange, but it will become easier. Most of the time, they are words we have been told by others, and we repeat them until these words are all we know and become a part of our identity.

If those thoughts are from *Shaytan*, however, that voice has only one agenda, and that is not to protect us, but to destroy us.

I remember when I had a difficult time trying to overcome the loud and mean voice in my head. It felt overwhelming and exhausting as it permeated my life and seemed to ruin the moments I wanted to enjoy. After a long time, I remembered I had some obligatory fasts to make up, and one day I fasted. Whilst fasting I observed the voices, and it was as if they had become quiet behind a veil, so much so that I could think clearly for the first time in a long time.

I would never have imagined something such as fasting would help me with this, but as I thought about it, it made sense. Fasting helps us to gain self-control and in doing so, it trains the soul and the mind, giving them a strength over the parts which can overcome us. And this helps in both the thoughts from the self and the thoughts from *Shaytan*.

THE SHADOW SELF

A shadow is an interesting thing. It can provide us with ease from the burning sun when we take refuge under a tree. Or we can let the shadows inside of us darken everything as we give into them. We cannot escape our shadows, but we can be aware of them, and this awareness is a kind of light which stops the shadows from controlling us.

In the context of our blinders, our shadows are our untamed desires. When they are untamed, left to themselves, fed, and obeyed, they become the root of our sins.

Desires in Islam are not only accepted but respected so much so that in heaven we are said to have all that we desire. However, there are boundaries around them, as with everything. Like the shadow, desires can become a place of refuge — of survival even, or we can become slaves to them, especially when there is an open wound waiting for something to fill it.

The following four qualities are the foundation of the major sins[62] and they typically follow in order, but we can hop from stage to stage. Every human has these qualities.

CATTLE QUALITIES

This is when we give in to the lowest of our desires and all we do is enjoy life's pleasures and nothing else. As we mentioned above, the desires we enjoy are not inherently condemnable, and in fact are crucial to our survival as humans. When done in moderation, the fulfilling of our desires becomes an act of worship. However, the problem is when we go to extremes. The people who fall into this stage are not evil, but they are similar to cattle. Due to this part of our shadow, we can fall into major sins like adultery, drinking alcohol, and so on.

PREDATORY QUALITIES

This is where our cattle qualities have become so extreme that they have a power over us, so much so that we will assault and attack people or things to get our fix. Some are more prone to these qualities, but we may not

(CONTINUED ON PAGE 95)

(CONTINUED FROM PAGE 94)

see it because predators might express it more covertly. Others might not express it at all, except through the feeling in their hearts that they would hurt another to get what they want, but because of their lack of boldness, they don't show it. The major sins from this are murder and mental or physical assault.

DEVILISH QUALITIES

These are the people who want to see others hurt, even if it doesn't benefit them. They enjoy pain for the sake of pain, and the major sins from this are stirring up enmity between people, being a talebearer, spying on people, and so on.

One of the most notoriously known qualities of the devil is his arrogance, which comes from an inflated ego.

Ego is hard to catch when it is unhealthy. When we talk about our weaknesses, we can notice the obvious things like being lazy, or loving a chocolate cake all day and every day (even for breakfast), and how that just isn't a good thing. With an unhealthy ego, however, we enter a victim mentality, where everyone else is the problem.

You may have heard that there is a rise in narcissism today. A narcissist is a person who has little self-awareness and overly admires themselves, thinking the world revolves around them. No matter the type of narcissist or the reason for being this way, their bloated ego always comes from a place of insecurity, and the scary thing is, we all have some level of narcissism inside of us.

The enjoyments of feeding a bloated ego are the hardest to give up because the ego demands. It shouts. It can be mean. Or too nice. It is controlling and subjective. Chaotic. Like Scrooge, it comes from a mindset of scarcity. It

(CONTINUED ON PAGE 96)

(CONTINUED FROM PAGE 95)

is the judgmental part of us, so desperate for validation. That is the inflated ego, the stark opposite of the Woke self.

The Woke Woman has internal validation so she doesn't need it from anyone else. Her state is one of abundance, her energy is bright, and she is gentle and kind, yet strong and virtuous. She doesn't try to compete with others and when she does, she catches herself because her Woke voice is clear and she knows how to listen to it. She is drawn, meaning she is carried in a flow toward her purpose, through the good times and the bad. And when she needs to be, she is driven, meaning she is assertive and works toward that purpose. She is in balance, authentic and curious.

This is a very different way of being, compared to coming from a place of a bloated ego. The more we do things from that place, the more we feel like we need to do. The more we feel we need to be. Until we become our everything, and in the worst case, we think we take the place of God.

Ego itself, however, is not a bad thing. It is a sense of self, and everyone needs a sense of self. The bloated part comes from ignorance + self-conceit + self-deceit. To bring it back into balance, we must gain knowledge with humility + practice of bettering the self. We will dive deeper into this in the next chapter.

WANTING TO BE GOD

This is when someone wants the qualities of Allah. For instance, some people crave everlasting life, which is not necessarily bad, but when we disobey Allah through it, it can become dangerous. Others want to be worshipped,

(CONTINUED ON PAGE 97)

(CONTINUED FROM PAGE 96)

which we see with most dictators today and throughout history. These people are the worst of us who will use their power to destroy and kill so they can be accepted as gods to the people.

We can remove these blinders by being aware of our shadow and its inclinations. Once aware, we can then spiritually train ourselves, a concept which we will talk about in the next chapter.

IN THE NAME OF BEING REAL

There is a movement in the wellness community toward being true to ourselves. However, we have many parts to ourselves, and amongst these are our shadow self and our wounded self. Being true to ourselves — being real — isn't always being real to the best version of ourselves.

For years I have been trying to be authentic to myself and I have learned that being authentic is an incomplete sentence. However, being authentic to the best version of myself completes that sentence, and it completes me.

The influences around us and within us can so easily sway our emotions that it becomes hard to hear that Woke voice within us. Islam and the practices that bind us to it free this part of us from all the clutter and conjecture, allowing us to taste the sweetness of what it means to be whole, to be Woke.

When we do what we are truly meant to do, we will find that the love is reciprocated, and doors open in ways we could never imagine. There is a well-known saying that the teacher comes when the student is ready, and when we break out of the cocoons of our conditioned ideals and unhealthy familiar patterns, we are ready to embrace the meaning of life at our core. Our passions become our mission, and though what we love might not seem to love us straight away, with training, our bodies will grow and learn to do what becomes natural, the same way we had to learn how to talk, walk and eat.

INSPIRED BY THE DEVIL

How can we know if we are inspired by the devil, or Allah, or our own goodness within? The rule of thumb is that if an inspiration takes you away from Allah, it is either from you or from *Shaytan*. The devil can inspire us in different ways, and one is by whispering half-truths to fortune tellers, a concept we discussed in the chapter of Spiritual Astuteness. Another way is by entering our hearts through open doorways.[63] The following are some of the doorways to the heart.

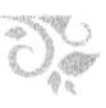

ENVY

This is when we think too much of other people and we compare ourselves to them. Comparison, however, is important to develop as humans. When we were babies, we had to compare the difference between milk and water, between mother and father, between pain and comfort. Comparing is natural; however, for many reasons, this comparison can be misused. Our parents might have constantly compared us to our siblings, or our teachers to our friends. And then there is the media which is full of filters, so the natural way of looking becomes plain and boring, and the photoshopped bodies and faces look magnificent. This may cause us to envy the way the models and influencers look.

To recognize if we are envious or not, we can observe our actions. Some signs of the envier within is when we don't want to share the good that someone has done, or when we gossip about people. Another sign is enjoying the misfortune of others.

We can remove this blinder by being aware of it and doing the opposite of what we are inclined to do toward

(CONTINUED ON PAGE 99)

(CONTINUED FROM PAGE 98)

that person. If we want to gossip, instead we can speak beautifully about them. I have added some resources in the back to help with this.

There is also a powerful verse in the Quran which is a prayer to Allah to ask Him to help us with this.

"And those who came after them say: 'Our Lord! Forgive us and our brethren who have preceded us in Faith and put not in our hearts any hatred against those who have believed. Our Lord! You are indeed full of kindness, Most Merciful.'"

Quran[64]

COVETOUSNESS

This is a kind of greed which makes us blind to the light of insight because our eyes are drawn to all the other flashing lights. When we are overly attached to something, such as material things, or even people, this becomes an unhealthy emotional attachment. In extremes it can lead us down a road of doom and gloom.

Emotions themselves are good and they signal deeper issues within us; however, when we are unaware of them, we can be consumed by them.

The difference between true passion and addiction is the light of passion rekindles things, while the light of addiction incinerates everything[65].

This covetousness can also be for people, where we love them to extremes, and our desire becomes obsession where we will do anything for their love and attention.

To want nice things is not bad, but when our sense of self is hollow, we will try and fill it with things that

(CONTINUED ON PAGE 100)

(CONTINUED FROM PAGE 99)

are unfulfilling in themselves. Our emotions become an invitation for *Shaytan* to come through this doorway to our hearts.

ANGER

The army of the heart are our limbs and when our hearts become weakened by anger, our limbs become the devil's playground. There are three types of anger: negligent, extreme and moderate/just.

Negligent: This is where a person lacks anger, and the things that should make them angry don't, such as a man letting other men flirt with his wife.

Extreme: This is where anger conquers the person, so they are unable to control their reaction and feel compelled to act, even if it breaks the bounds of Islam.

Moderate and just: Anger is not a bad thing. When we push it down and ignore it, it does not leave, but becomes so that it can build into resentment, which is victim anger. Anger can also cause our bodies to get sick. My point is that anger never really leaves us; it must be released in a healthy way. An unhealthy way might be covert, where a person is unaware that they are being passive aggressive because as children they were not allowed to express their anger. Righteous anger is not covert, nor is it buried in resentment. It is when we are angry for the right reason, and we use it to our benefit rather than allow it to control us. There are many ways we can do this, such as using the four pillars of wisdom: knowledge, forbearance, justice, and deliberation. We can also

(CONTINUED ON PAGE 101)

(CONTINUED FROM PAGE 100)

stabilize our state of anger by calming our bodies before we react. A wonderful way to do this is through grounding ourselves with water, such as making wudu, and changing the position we are in. When we are in a state of forbearance, where our emotions are not at peaks, we can think about the situation and the best way to go about it. There is an excellent article in the Look Deeper section by Sarah Sultan which goes much deeper into this.

When we remove these doorways of the devil through spiritual training, he can no longer live in our hearts. Instead, he is limited to fleeting thoughts. The devil is like a thief, and when we shine a light on our flaws and become aware of his presence, like all thieves, he will run.

OTHER PEOPLE'S TOXIC VIBES

Once we reach a state of being Woke, we will find that people might change toward us. Some will come closer and embrace, the true versions of us, quirks and all, but others will begin to show negativity.

Thankfully there is plenty of material out there on how to recognize negativity from people, and we also have our internal nudges which tell us something might not be right. These nudges give our hearts a feeling of heaviness, and whether we like it or not, the way people act can really affect us.

I had this experience myself, many times, and I pondered for years on how to deal with it. One day, I read a verse in the Quran, and for the first time a clarity came over me.

I want to be clear that this is what the verse meant to me, from a human reflection, and not a scholarly understanding.

*"Kind words and forgiveness are better than charity followed by injury.
And Allah is Self-Sufficient, Most Forbearing."*

Quran[66]

When I read this, I saw how Allah is rich and not in need of people and yet, He is the Most Forbearing. I saw the importance of how as humans, we must have a strong sense of self, and in the case of negativity from people, to be forbearing and experience that wave of emotions, rather than peaks, helps us see things more clearly.

The idea here is not to be unreactive and let people trespass our bounds. Rather, we should strive to be in a place where we can be objective and decide with insight what the best course of action is, without the need to fill ourselves with something that is missing, which might lead to treating others unjustly or letting ourselves be treated unjustly. We could decide whether to make our needs known or let the negativity slide. We could decide whether we want to keep being in the company of the person, or if it is better for our mental health to stay away from their provocation. I believe that people can grow and improve, which is why I am writing this book. But I also know that there is only so much that I can do personally, and it is up to them to do the rest.

Wow. We've covered so much in this chapter! Most of the blinders we have spoken about are faced by being aware of them, and from there, when we make the intention to grow, we can then ask the question of how we can better ourselves. The answer will come *if Allah wills*. In the next and final chapter of Part II, we will do this work together, you and I, so rest if you need, and I'll see you there.

AT A GLANCE

We have parts of us that can lead us to be blind to the truth.

The first step toward helping ourselves is to be aware of those parts.

one small thing

Add a day more than you already have for fasting voluntary fasts.

insights

CHAPTER 10

THE PLEDGE OF THE WOKE

In this chapter, you and I will take a pledge together as sisters in faith. In taking this pledge, I would love to hold your hand as a support, but because we are not together in person, I want you to hold your own hands together as a support for yourself. This is a powerful and spiritual pledge, one which, by the permission of Allah, will change everything if we do it with intention.

When something wonderful is about to happen, or we are doing something new, a fear might arise, sometimes paralyzing us as we stay in the same soil which no longer feeds us to grow into the beautiful trees we can become. Our brain loves familiarity, even if this means that, for instance, we stay in an abusive relationship because our abuser is someone we have always known. We stay as we are because we know what to expect; it helped us once, didn't it? We stay because to do anything different would shatter the truths we have come to believe about ourselves.

This fear to grow as people might show up as fear of failure, "What's the point, I'm not going to get the job anyway!" or fear of success, "What if I lose all the people I love if I take that job?" but ultimately both fear of success and fear of failure come from the fear of change.

When we are unaware of where all the conflicting feelings are coming from, we become blind to the busybody work of self-sabotage. For me, it shows up when I overwork and end up feeling burned out. I then realize, after stepping back, that I missed the whole point my work and now I physically can't do anything. For others, it can show up when they're getting to know a potential spouse and everything is just perfect — until they blurt out everything about their blotchy past, telling themselves, "This is me, I'm being real!" when deep down, they know it's going to scare the potential spouse off.

Self-sabotage can be sneaky. If during our pledge, you hit a metaphorical wall, be gentle and observe yourself. Self-sabotage, however harsh its inner critic, or stubbornness in its urge to do something (or not), isn't trying to hurt us. In fact, it is trying to protect us, and it is not acting from our true self, but another part of us, which lives in fear.

Everything we have learned thus far is to strengthen our true and best self, and this is the opposite of where self-sabotage comes from. Our true and best self acts from a place of love for Allah, and strength in knowing our Big Why. We are curious, open, and see the world with clarity. This is what it means to be self-led.

Yes, it is terrifying to step into the unknown, but here is a truth bomb: change, my lovely, is the only thing that is never going to change. And this cannot be bought into fruition by a few positive affirmations in the mirror every morning. True change includes our whole mindset, and it needs practice. This is where our pledge will help you begin that praiseworthy and heavenly journey, if Allah wills.

It is ok to pause. It is ok to breathe. It is ok to go slowly. The key is that you keep going and that you don't need to prove yourself to anyone. Now let's make a pledge.

1. I WILL ACCEPT THE TRUTH WITH SINCERITY.

Our hardest truth is that we have flaws, but when we are sincere in our growth, humbleness meets us, and we not only gain understanding of the world, but also our place within it — including the good we bring and the not so good. There are four ways we can uncover our flaws[67].

➤ Ask a person of knowledge and insight about your apparent strengths and weaknesses. It has become rare to find a person like this, but when you do, their advice is so valuable because their lens is much deeper than anyone else's.

➤ Surround yourself with righteous companions. These people will tell you the truth (in a nice way of course!), even if it means you won't like it — or them. It is so easy to be around people who flatter you and tell you that your imperfections are gold, but be careful of a person who over-compliments you. You need friends who can tell you when you are not doing so well and when you find these special souls, keep them close.

➤ What do our enemies say about us? This one is hard. A friend might tell us what we need to hear and feel sadness because they know it hurts us, but our enemies are more ruthless. The harsher the truth, the bigger the damage. It is important to take this advice while utilizing the four pillars of wisdom: knowledge, forbearance, justice, and deliberation. These will help us be more objective with what our enemies say about us so we can determine what is true and what is just plain mean.

➤ Mingle with people and observe blameworthy qualities and learn from them. It is important to do this from a place of curiosity and not judgement.

If we find that we have flaws — which we will — we might become aware of certain behaviors we have been doing where we hurt someone without realizing. In these times, it is important to ask Allah for forgiveness and guidance. The greatest act of repentance is not repeating the sin, and as long as we are alive, we can keep trying to work on ourselves.

2. I WILL VISUALIZE MY SPIRITUAL GOALS.

If there was one thing you wanted to do more of — or less of — in your life, what would it be? Begin there. And with time, add more, but be realistic about it.

Included in this spiritual goal are things like comparing yourself to others and healing from trauma. When we work on bettering and healing ourselves, we work on the biases which have kept us from growing spiritually, emotionally, and physically for so long. We remove those parts which have blocked us from our true self, and our *fitra* becomes strong.

3. I WILL WORK WITH MYSELF LOVINGLY.

This means to be kinder to ourselves, and to work with our bodies in a way that shows we care about them. This means to not overwork or engage is excessive negative self-talk. It also means to work with our monthly flow.

Working with our bodies means listening to them. This can be something as simple as making sure we eat breakfast or sleep when we are tired, despite all the work we "have" to get done. In the end, the work will get done *God willing*, but it shouldn't be at the expense of hurting our bodies which belong to Allah.

The greatest self-care is to give our bodies what they need, even if others might consider it a privilege. If you need to be alone to have an epsom salt bath-and read a good novel, then do it!

When I say listen to your bodies, I don't mean the appetite self, the self which is driven by only desire. It is important to have balance, and this is where our spiritual goals, such as fasting regularly or waking up through the night to pray to Allah, will help us.

Another way to work with our bodies is to take breaks between daily activities to process the events. Sometimes after meetings we leave feeling exhausted because the conversation was so heavy. Generally, we just continue our day, beginning another activity without taking a break which we need if we are to allow our body to process what happened or was said in the meeting.

These breaks within our day are crucial to self-care, and the perfect way to do this is through our five daily prayers. The most fulfilling life is one where we are present, and this begins in our prayers. Everything becomes aligned to the state we are in when we pray. When we take our time, remain present, reflect over every act and every word in praise of our Lord which reminds us of our purpose, then not only do our prayer becomes a place of refuge, a sanctuary of peace and rest, but our lives become easier too. It is during our prayers where we reconnect to Allah and reconnect to the self.

When we bow our head to the ground, we are grounded. As we raise our palms, we are in submission to Allah, the Greatest one, greater than all our problems. As we prostrate, we fall into the fetal position where our bodies feel safest, as they did when we were in our mother's womb.

All these acts are powerful, and they not only remind the mind of what truly matters, but the body, which also has a memory and finds ease in the prayers to Allah. Praying on time is the greatest act of self-care. It helps us process, revive our energy, and fill our hearts with peace.

4. I WILL IMPROVE MYSELF IN INCREMENTS.

The closer we are to Allah, the more we feel we need to achieve, and a sure way to self-sabotage is to raise the bar so high that we cannot reach it. In visualizing our spiritual goals, I asked you to choose just one thing that you want to do to improve spiritually. The idea is to do small but consistent acts, and with time, we add to them.

Though Allah made us with His perfect planning, we are not expected to be perfect. He does, however, love for us to work toward excellence,[68] and we can't do that if we try to do and be everything.

So again, please be kinder to yourself. It is ok to rest and honor your limits. You know yourself better than any other human, so only you can truly honor yourself by doing the work in a way that will have a positive long-term impact on you.

5. I WILL HAVE ROLE MODELS WHOM I CAN LOOK UP TO AND LEARN FROM.

The greatest role model is our final Messenger ﷺ, and his life was an example to us. I have left some resources in the back for you to learn more about him ﷺ his mercy, his hardship, his balance, and his way.

In the spaces of greatness sprinkled throughout this book, there are some more amazing role models who can inspire us to do good. I chose these women because they were the best of our nation, better than any modern-day celebrity. In our own Muslim community, there have been instances where an influential teacher either said or did something wrong, and thousands of people who had attached their faith to him or her and ended up losing motivation, or worse, their own faith.

Islam is not attached to a person; it is the truth, and the truth will always be on the side of Allah. We humans make mistakes.

Abdullah ibn Masood (RA):

"Whoever wants to follow a path, let him follow the path of one who has died, for the living are not safe from fitnah. I mean the Companions of Muhammad ﷺ They were the best of this ummah: the purest in heart, the deepest in knowledge and the most straightforward. Allah chose them to accompany His Prophet and establish His religion, so recognize their status and follow in their footsteps and adhere as much as you can to their example of conduct and attitude, for they followed true guidance. "[69]

It is easy to fall into deep admiration for people who use their platforms for good, and may Allah bless them in this. But remember the pillar of wisdom, forbearance, which means to love in moderation and hate in moderation because one day, the one you love might become the one you hate, and the one you hate might become the one you love.

6. I WILL NOT COMPARE MYSELF TO OTHERS. THIS IS MY JOURNEY. I FOLLOW MY PATH.

There are so many versions of the "right" way. It is easy to get lost in hustle culture — especially if we want to become published authors. With so many motivational influencers available, we can easily fall into the doom scroll, comparing ourselves to others' wealth, beauty, confidence, handsome hubby and so on.

Here is a principle which will help with this.

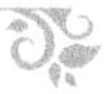

Look to those higher than you in closeness to Allah and not to those who have more than you in material gains. And look to those who have less than you in material wealth to be grateful for what you do have.

THE BLUEPRINT TO BEING WOKE:

I have also attached this quote to the beginning of your book for easy reference. Up until now and everything after in this book can be summarized in the following blueprint to understanding inspiration.

"The more a servant employs their intellect and acts upon their knowledge and purifies their actions through complete devotion and their conscience becomes purer and they reflect with the sight of intellect, the intelligence of the soul and the acumen of the heart and grow their certainty and abolish their doubts and tame their senses with prophetic etiquettes and reign their thoughts with watchfulness of the divine and avoid lying in speech or action until truthfulness becomes their hometown from which ostentation and self-connectedness are expelled and show need and brokenness before their Lord and disavow their influence and power and commit to service of their Lord and observe the sanctity of proper etiquettes and watch the bounds and adhere to the Sunnah and run away from innovation, the recognition will be elevated and their insight will be sharpened and things hidden from the sights will be disclosed to them and they become the people of lofty rankings by virtue of their gratitude, that results in increase and abundance"

Ibn Taymiyyah

Great change does not happen in a day, or a month. To become the woman you want to be takes consistency and intention. No matter how small your steps seem, you are still moving forward. You are a brilliant woman, and the world needs more people who truly want to be better humans — in a healthy way. Please acknowledge and celebrate each step, and may Allah make your path one of ease and blessings. Ameen.

Congratulations, you have finished the second part of your book! In the next part, we will talk about your vision and working on your masterpiece, using everything we have learned. Take a break, give yourself what you need, and then let's dive in!

AT AL GLACE

Change is scary.

Take small steps towards change.

Be kind to yourself.

one small thing

Choose one thing you want to add to your day or week. Add it into your routine and practice it regularly for a month. Every month, add something small to your spiritual goal.

insights

Part III

VISION

This is the result.
Of growth.
Of self.
Of truth.
Of belief.
It is the path of a believer whose eyes expand,
with a heart which gives thanks.
Greater than the borders inside our paper sheets.
Penciling words whose audience is heaven.
Decorating thrones above rivers which flow
It is the masterpiece who creates a masterpiece.
It is you.
The product of purpose
Of depth
Of excellence
Of balance
Peace.
It is time to write.
To record.
To reflect.
To tell.
To transform.
Now blossom.

CHAPTER 11

GATHERING THE TROOPS

The title of this chapter refers to a term which is commonly used in story structure where at the very end, the protagonist gathers all the troops and uses them in the final act of overcoming the internal or external antagonist. It is the finale with a pop, and the lessons of the book work together for a satisfying and enthralling end.

Our gathering of the troops is not a finale, but it is the final part of being Woke, where we come full circle to our tongue, heart, and limbs as a team toward our Big Why. It is to use all we have learned about Allah, our relationship with Him, and ourselves. It is to create a piece of work which is truly visionary in the sense that every word we write goes beyond this life and becomes a testimony for our good on the Day of Judgement. This is the impact of the Woke Writer. And it all begins with our intention.

The most powerful thing we have within us is the ability to harness a pure intention. Imagine a superhero trying to get a grip on their power which is their gateway to success, to defeating all enemies and rising above the world. Martyrs have been destined for hell, and people who have lived a life of sin but fed a small animal have been destined for heaven, based on their intention. Intention in Islam is a heavy trust, and once our hearts are sincere in tandem with acting upon the authentic way of our final Messenger ﷺ , we have tapped into something truly great. When we can act with sincere intention and supplicate with a heart guided by it, we don't need to call upon the power within ourselves as most superheroes do. Instead we call upon the One who has power over all the universes and all that is within them. This is where our success lies.

The heart is also the home of faith and motivation. It is the place where Allah's inspiration enters, a refuge for insight and where we recognize what is good and bad. Within our heart, every action we do becomes high stakes because our heart is ever turning. The literal meaning for the heart in Arabic is *qalb*, which means "to turn." So, we must be constantly vigilant in doctoring our hearts to turn back to faith and to revive our intention.

It is important to have a sincere intention before writing, but also during, and after we finish. Once we have our intention, it is time to start the process of finding our Small Why which is the means toward achieving our Big Why. We can do this through the following steps.

STEP ONE: TAKE CARE OF YOUR HEART

When we build our resilience against bad through the force of good, our good deeds give us the strength and vigor to continue. We must maintain our hearts and the good inside them. This means to constantly check back with our intention and reflect over what makes our heart feel wide or constricted through asking questions like, "Is my intention waning? Why? Did I hear something which clouded it in a subtle but dangerous way? Did I do something which seemed small, but it created a veil over my heart? Why does my heart feel numb, far from Allah?"

When we gather our troops from Part I and Part II, which allows us to see things from a strong foundation through a clear lens, we will be drawn to good. It is a law of Allah that good attracts good.

STEP TWO: FOLLOW YOUR HEART

Now that you have checked your heart, it is the time to ask what you are drawn to. What excites you? What are you good at? You can be multi-talented, like the Islamic scholars of the past who mastered numerous disciplines, wrote many books, taught hundreds of students, and fought in wars.

As writers, it is important to embrace all parts of our talents: the creative part which shines in the messages we craft, the technical part of refining our craft, and the social part where we share our masterpieces with confidence and purpose.

If you are unsure about your strengths and which type of writing you enjoy most, give yourself full permission to explore different genres and types of writing.

STEP THREE: GIVE SPACE TO YOUR SMALL WHY

Our Small Why is our how to our Big Why. With our passions, some good questions to ask are: "How can I use my passion to please Allah? To make a positive difference in the world? To be of service or benefit to others?"

The best writers are the most resourceful. They can use seemingly unrelated talents and passions so that everything fits together to create meaningful masterpieces. You might love gardening and feel guilty when you do it because "real writers write a lot." But if that gardening nurtures your connection to Earth, grounding you and helping you to be in a healthy mental space, it serves your writing much more than writing for hours on empty.

You might also have a dream to write full-time but feel reluctant about taking that leap. For now, try not to put pressure on yourself and just enjoy the process. Your job is to give your writing space, and with time and loyalty to your craft, the pieces of the puzzle will come together.

If you decide to take that leap to becoming a full-time writer or creative, know that Allah is Ar Razak, which means He is the Provider, and your provision has already been decreed. We will always get what is destined for us, no matter what we do. So ... why not do what you love?

STEP FOUR: BE READY FOR
WHEREVER THE JOURNEY TAKES YOU

We spoke about this in the chapter of surrender — to be ready to change direction and accept what comes. As humans, we change constantly, and that means our interests might change or evolve. This grand idea of finding the ultimate thing which is our "purpose" sometimes stops us from our true path. We can become lost in what we think things should be and lose who we are. Remember our Big Why and that any effort toward it is never a loss, but a gain.

As you begin to explore yourself and your passions, you will know which troops to gather for that moment. You might need to pull on the pillars of wisdom, through gaining knowledge of your craft or taking time away from your manuscript to deliberate and gain more objectivity. You might have a question about a story and whether it is aligned with the Quran and Sunnah, so you visit the highest of the hierarchy of wisdom to find the answer. You ask Allah and look to the way of His Messenger ﷺ as the believers who have knowledge. You might even ask someone to critique your work and give you some pointers on the flaws.

When the answers come, you might surrender to a new direction, or, through a good omen or sincere advice. Alternatively, you might feel peace in your heart in knowing that your current direction is correct. The most important thing to realize is, Allah has made you with purpose, and with Allah you will never lose.

AT A GLANCE

Our hearts are the home of creativity, intention, faith, and motivation and must be constantly maintained.

Our passions are not coincidental.

With Allah we will never lose.

one small thing

Dedicate a period of time each week to writing. Even if it is just one hour, it is important that you make space for this. Increase the amount of time when it feels right.

insights

CHAPTER 12

THE WOKE WRITER

Everything we have learned up until now has been a step toward our most authentic selves through knowing our Lord and knowing ourselves. And doing the work. From now, all that comes from you will be a product of you. Your work has always been a product of you. It is a part of you, and it is your greatest mirror, showing your uniqueness, beauty, and spiritual consciousness.

However, this doesn't mean that we won't make mistakes. Even when we approach our work with the best of intentions and improving ourselves, we can still fall into grey areas. For example, if you are writing a novel, and you have some things within which you might be worried about, it's time to check on your Woke heart and listen to its calling. Gather your troops and use the ones that will help you overcome the block which is created from the grey area.

Speaking of blocks, we can't talk about writing and not mention writer's block. There are many opinions on writer's block, so I want to be clear that this is my understanding of it. There are two kinds of writer's block.

➤ **Writer's Block:** This is when the blinders on our being Woke are stopping us from continuing. A big one is past trauma, and this shows up in our writing in the most unpredictable ways such as perfectionism, procrastination, fear of writing, and even guilt. Many times, this is because we have been told by those whose opinion weighed heavily on us that our writing is a waste of time. Or that we should be doing other things that a good Muslim woman should do, such as maintaining the home.

Everything is about balance, and when we have gathered the troop of wisdom, we will be able to know where everything goes, meaning that our priorities will be clear to us: Allah, ourselves, our homes. When I say ourselves, I mean taking care of ourselves and making sure we are in a place of strength. This means taking personal time, and that time might be writing. I can vouch as a mother with small children that we can carve out time for the things we love — for our writing, even if it is twenty minutes in the day. It is those things that make us fuller and happier in whatever role we are in. So, take care of yourself and don't feel guilty about it.

➤ **Writer's Breath:** I wouldn't really count this as writer's block — more of a temporary writer's block. Sometimes we just need a break, a simple walk, or some time away from our writing.

WHAT KIND OF WRITER ARE YOU?

Some of us love to plan our writing, and others love to go with the flow. Some like to write at night, and others like to write in the morning. In the first draft of this book, I implemented a very specific writing routine, and over time, I have learned that we all struggle with different things, and we all have our own way of doing things. And the most important thing for you as a writer is to honor that. That takes practice in writing in different styles, using different processes, or writing different genres.

When I first started my novel, the only place I could write was on a busy subway on my way to Manhattan, whilst six months pregnant. I started to feel like a penguin from waddling around New York City, but after each writing session, I felt like a purposeful penguin. I finished a whole draft on those trips! Later as I fell into the routine of being home more and waking up early on my baby's schedule, I began to write earlier and I found that my mind was its most clear and my writing was its most … *me*, in those early hours.

My point is that you too have your own processes, and your way is not wrong just because it is different from mine. One thing I must say however is that there are many blessings in the morning hours, and our Prophet Muhammed ﷺ made a special supplication for the morning person.

It was narrated from Sakhr Al-Ghamidi that the Messenger of Allah ﷺ said: 'O Allah, bless my nation in their early mornings (i.e., what they do early in the morning).'[70]

WRITING ON OUR WOMANLY FLOW

During our womanly cycles, there are certain strengths we have in each phase, and we can use them in our writing. The first part of our cycles — menstruation, follicular and ovulation — are more immersed in the right brain, which we spoke about in the chapter of Mental Astuteness. Here we are more intuitive and creative. The second half of our cycle, the luteal phase, is more in the left brain, so we are more detail-oriented and focused on achieving tasks. Our menstrual cycle harnesses the strength of both the right and the left brain, so it is a good time to evaluate everything and decide how to move forward.

PHASE 1: MENSTRUATION,
SUPERPOWER: REFLECTION

In relation to writing, you want to combine the left brain and the right brain. Menstruation is a really good time to think about your masterpiece. Are you content with its direction, or does something feel off? This is a time to evaluate everything and from this we can analyze and strategize.

PHASE 2: FOLLICULAR PHASE,
SUPERPOWER: CREATIVITY

This is an ideal time to brainstorm and record your ideas. You're going to have some amazing ones, God willing. It is also a good time to say *yes* to new things — like that writers' conference! Creatively, as we said, you are most in the right brain. This is my favorite phase because I feel more open to new ideas and new beginnings. You might even have a skip in your step because it's like spring just came around. Woo-hoo!

PHASE 3: OVULATION,
SUPERPOWER: MAGNETIC

Creatively, you are in the right brain. The verbal and social centers of the brain are stimulated, and this means it is a great time to network with other writers and like-minded people (or not like-minded, but good to connect with). If you want to traditionally publish your work, it's a good time to query agents. If you want to talk about your work, jump on some podcasts like *The Strange Inc Show* (the link to this is the resources section in the 'Look Deeper 'section) who would love to hear your experiences as a Muslim woman writer.

PHASE 4: LUTEAL,
SUPERPOWER: TASK-ORIENTED

Towards the end of the phase, you might feel sad, and when we are sad, we notice details more. To make this a strength, use your skill for detail to edit your work. This task phase is the longest for a good reason, and Allah created us perfectly, so this is the time to check off you're to-do list. Stay focused! Creatively you are more in the left brain, so grammar and punctuation come more easily to you.

If you have passed the stage of having womanly cycles, you can still harness your feminine power. Research has found that postmenopausal women are more creative and have more time to focus on themselves.

Though we said that we all have different writing processes, if you want to publish a book, there are general steps that most writers will go through.

BE WOKE

Yes, it is true that some writers who have published many books might not have put this as number one. But you, my sister are gloriously not most writers and for you, as a Muslim woman who is powerful and authentic to your best you, is a priority.

BRAINSTORM

Be open and let your curiosity flow. Is there an image you keep seeing or a story you wish you could tell? Maybe it's the ending, or maybe it's the beginning. There is no order here, so let your heart and mind explore.

OUTLINE – OR DON'T

Either way, it is always good to have a rough direction of where you're going, especially for nonfiction work.

THE FIRST DRAFT

For this endeavor you want to be in the right brain, as it is all about creativity. You might write your draft in seemingly random parts, and that is totally ok. This draft should be done for your eyes only because it is such a tender part of the writing process, and your ideas are finding their place on the page. The last thing we need is for someone to tell us a different idea would be better, or our ideas don't work. Close the metaphorical door and write what your heart tells you. It will be a total mess, and again, that is totally ok. One thing you want to do, however, is to write consistently and hold that space we talked about in the previous chapter. You can honor that space literally by doing things like having a special, antique-looking writing lamp, or savoring a custom coffee

(CONTINUED ON PAGE 128)

(CONTINUED FROM PAGE 127)

during your writing. Keep in mind that this honoring of your space and actions is not a ritual in the sense of worship, but a habit which you are creating to nurture the writing process. Remember intention is everything to the Woke Writer.

TAKE SOME TIME AWAY

Once your first draft is finished, make sure to take some time away from your manuscript. Ideally it should be a few weeks or even months so that you can approach your work with fresh reader eyes.

APPROACH YOUR MANUSCRIPT WITH FRESH READER EYES

To do this, you can print your manuscript or read it in a different format. You can even sit in a different place from where you normally write. During this step, read your work as quickly as possible — preferably all in the same day — and then put it out of sight for a few more weeks.

PICK UP YOUR MANUSCRIPT AND BEGIN SELF-EDITING

When you read the manuscript with fresh reader eyes, this will give the subconscious part of your mind time to ponder things that stood out. When we pick up our manuscript for self-editing, there are two main processes we go through: big edits and small edits. The big edits are where we look at the structure of the piece, and if our first draft is all over the place, this is the part where we organize it. When the big edits are complete, then we work on the small edits which iron out the details to thread the book together. You will go through the self-editing process a few times, and the more the better. It is important

(CONTINUED ON PAGE 129)

(CONTINUED FROM PAGE 128)

to be patient with yourself and remember that even if it takes a few years to finish your book, those words will be read many more years after you die, God willing, so I'd say it's worth taking longer to finish if you need to. The editing phase is rooted in the left brain.

FIND A PROSPECTIVE READER TO GIVE FEEDBACK ON YOUR MANUSCRIPT

This would either be a beta reader or a critique partner. You can also join a critique circle, which Strange Inc. offers for Muslim women writers in their online community The Writers Block. The difference between the two is that if you want a firm deadline for the reader to finish your work, you will get a critique partner who offers their critique as a service. The best prospective reader is a writer themself who is interested in your genre. I would highly recommend that you don't ask a family member, friend, or anyone else who might have a conflict of interest in your work. Take your prospective reader's feedback with objectivity. A clue to an issue in your work is if more than one person comes back to you with the same comment.

GO PRO

Find a professional editor who will either do a big edit or a small edit, depending on what you feel you need. In more technical terms, a developmental editor will review your manuscript and make or suggest big edits, a copy editor will focus on the smaller edits such as sentence structure and grammar, and a proofreader will correct spelling and typos and any other mistakes before or after the final formatting of the book.

(CONTINUED ON PAGE 130)

(CONTINUED FROM PAGE 129)

FORMATTING

Before formatting, it would be helpful to print your edited manuscript and read it yourself, line by line, to catch any grammatical issues with your own eyes. Then send your work to a professional formatter to format it. They will return it to you, and you will read over the work and send revisions to them.

BOOK COVER DESIGN

You can do this simultaneously with the formatter, or even the editor. The book design is a very important part of publishing your book, and it is important to make sure it looks professional.

PUBLISH!

If you choose to go traditional, then steps 9, 10 and 11 above won't apply to you because the publisher would do all this for you. Instead, you would find a literary agent through a query letter, and that agent would approach prospective publishers on your behalf and try to sell your manuscript to them. If they accept your work, the publishing house would reserve the rights for your book, and you might receive an advance. You will get a small portion of royalties — commonly 10% — and the publisher gets the rest. Alternatively, you can self-publish where you manage your own book. The benefit of this is that you get all the royalties for it and reserve all rights. And finally, you can go through hybrid publishing, which is a merge between traditional and self-publishing. This is where the author and the publishing house partner to help the author finish their book. There would be a split in royalties, and the hybrid publisher serves as a guide for the author whilst the

(CONTINUED ON PAGE 131)

(CONTINUED FROM PAGE 130)

author reserves all rights to their own work.

All avenues have their advantages and disadvantages. As a writer, decide which things are most important to you. Do what you feel is most aligned with your goals.

MARKETING YOUR BOOK

Whatever avenue you go through to publish, you, as the author, are mostly responsible for your own marketing. A traditional or a hybrid publisher might help you with some parts, but you are the driving force behind it. It is important that you do what you are intuitively drawn toward. I know this isn't the common idea amongst writers who market. Some might claim that it's best to go all out, using every platform and every method possible. But I respectfully disagree. If you have the energy to be in all the places, doing all the things, then that is amazing, but if you don't, then that is totally ok too. This doesn't mean you don't market; it just means you choose the mode of sharing your book which works best for you. If you prefer to speak on podcasts and not be so visible in the eyes of people, then do you. If you can show up for an Instagram live every week, then do you. If you prefer Facebook, then use that. But the most important thing you want to take advantage of is your email list. That is where you will reach people who have taken a conscious step to enter your circle of interest in your message, and an inbox is very personal. You want to nurture that relationship with your audience through updates that you want to share, or even quotes from your book — get creative and most importantly, have fun with it! Another key thing to keep in mind is to have an author website where people can find your amazing work and learn more about you — the amazing author behind it.

As of this book's publication, the nonprofit publishing house Strange Inc. follows a hybrid model, offering comprehensive support throughout the writing process. From one-on-one writing coaching to critique partners, editing, and both book interior and exterior design, they are there every step of the way.

Congratulations, you have almost reached the end of this book! We as women and as Muslims have a great power of will within us, and when every part of us is working as one, toward our one purpose, our life and our work enter a state of flow. When we reach that station of flow, however, this will not be the end of our trials. Rather we will approach them in a way that is wise, and our work will reflect our highest self.

Next, we will look at a sample of a journal that will help you along your writing path. The hope is that you will be deliberate and intentional in your work, whilst honoring it. After the journal, in the final part of this book, I have shared some amazing resources which are helpful in looking deeper into everything we have covered, chapter by chapter.

Thank you for being here with me, and I pray Allah blesses and guides every word you write and makes it a testimony of greatness for you on the Day of Judgement. Ameen. I also want you to know that even if the whole world doesn't read your words — perhaps only a few, or maybe even none — that act of writing with meaning had an impact if it weighed heavily on your scales of good on The Day of Judgment, and that is what really mattered. I hate goodbyes; I never seem to be very good at them. So I will end with this: Only good can ever come from good.

"Is there any reward for good other than good?"[71]

AT A GLANCE

Our writing processes will differ because we each differ.

Study the steps writers go through to finish a book and adapt them to your own style.

A space for greatness

YOU

I'm holding this space for you, my sister in faith. You have come so far, and the fact you have kept reading shows a lot. I hope that you can fill the spaces that this world has, with words that are from a pure heart, inspired by Allah, within His bounds, so you can truly be free in the best and most authentic version of yourself. Your writing is important, and you are needed.

one small thing

Write your message to the world. Write.

insights

CHAPTER 13

YOUR JOURNAL

There are three sections in this journal, and I have created a template for you to follow in the first thirty days of writing- the average length of your cycle. However, just one cycle is not enough to study our patterns, so I urge you to keep at it, even when this journal here is finished. Use the template in that beautiful diary you bought or made from the chapter of Mental Asuteness. You don't have to write in your journal every day, but it would be great if you wrote on your dedicated writing days. Your reflections don't have to be super in-depth or long. Here is an example of my own:

October 17ᵗʰ 2021

Day two cycle

Today I finished reading my whole first draft! I read it in two days and it's about 50,000 words.

I read it with no judgement, but still my editing mind kept saying to cut things out. But I refocused and told myself to read the draft.

Now I will put it away for a week or so, and during my book days I will read another book in the same genre to see how the structure is.

I feel nervous about editing. Where do I begin? I have a good idea and I think I might even enjoy it. There's something fulfilling about putting things together.

And another …

November 21ˢᵗ, 2021

Day 8 cycle

I added some major changes which bought the threads of the story together. I think everything fits. I wonder how much of the original draft I'm sticking to? Or if the major plot holes and writing the big changes down made a difference? They were useful in telling me what I have and what I need changing.

We shall see.

In your writing journal, there are three main parts:

Date and Cycle Day

Spiritual Temperature from 1-10

Reflections: This is where you can write about how you moved forward with your writing, even if there was an energy shift where you felt inspired about a part of your writing. You can also share lessons of what you learned about yourself as a writer, what works for you, and what doesn't.

one small thing

Add the "one small things" at the end of each chapter to your diary, including the layout of the following journal.

DATE: _________________________________ DAY _____ OF MY CYCLE

SPIRITUAL TEMPERATURE:

1   2   3   4   5   6   7   8   9   10

(COLD)   (HOT)

REFLECTIONS:

____

____

____

____

____

____

____

____

____

____

____

____

____

____

____

____

DATE: _________________________________ DAY _____ OF MY CYCLE

SPIRITUAL TEMPERATURE:

1   2   3   4   5   6   7   8   9   10

REFLECTIONS:

____

____

____

____

____

____

____

____

____

____

____

____

____

____

____

____

____

DATE: _________________________________ DAY _____ OF MY CYCLE

SPIRITUAL TEMPERATURE:

1   2   3   4   5   6   7   8   9   10

REFLECTIONS:

____

____

____

____

____

____

____

____

____

____

____

____

____

____

____

____

DATE: _______________________________ DAY _____ OF MY CYCLE

SPIRITUAL TEMPERATURE:

1   2   3   4   5   6   7   8   9   10

REFLECTIONS:

____

____

____

____

____

____

____

____

____

____

____

____

____

____

____

____

DATE: ____ DAY _______ OF MY CYCLE

SPIRITUAL TEMPERATURE:

1   2   3   4   5   6   7   8   9   10

REFLECTIONS:

____

____

____

____

____

____

____

____

____

____

____

____

____

____

____

____

DATE: _________________________________ DAY _____ OF MY CYCLE

SPIRITUAL TEMPERATURE:

1   2   3   4   5   6   7   8   9   10

REFLECTIONS:

____

____

____

____

____

____

____

____

____

____

____

____

____

____

____

____

____

____

DATE: ____ DAY _______ OF MY CYCLE

SPIRITUAL TEMPERATURE:

1   2   3   4   5   6   7   8   9   10

REFLECTIONS:

____

____

____

____

____

____

____

____

____

____

____

____

____

____

____

DATE: _______________________________________ DAY _______ OF MY CYCLE

SPIRITUAL TEMPERATURE:

1   2   3   4   5   6   7   8   9   10

REFLECTIONS:

DATE: _______________________________________ DAY _______ OF MY CYCLE

SPIRITUAL TEMPERATURE:

1   2   3   4   5   6   7   8   9   10

REFLECTIONS:

DATE: _________________________________ DAY _____ OF MY CYCLE

SPIRITUAL TEMPERATURE:

1   2   3   4   5   6   7   8   9   10

REFLECTIONS:

____

____

____

____

____

____

____

____

____

____

____

____

____

____

____

____

____

____

DATE: _______________________________ DAY _____ OF MY CYCLE

SPIRITUAL TEMPERATURE:

1   2   3   4   5   6   7   8   9   10

REFLECTIONS:

DATE: _______________________________ DAY _____ OF MY CYCLE

SPIRITUAL TEMPERATURE:

1   2   3   4   5   6   7   8   9   10

REFLECTIONS:

____

____

____

____

____

____

____

____

____

____

____

____

____

____

____

____

____

DATE: ____ DAY _____ OF MY CYCLE

SPIRITUAL TEMPERATURE:

1   2   3   4   5   6   7   8   9   10

REFLECTIONS:

____

____

____

____

____

____

____

____

____

____

____

____

____

____

____

____

DATE: _________________________________ DAY _____ OF MY CYCLE

SPIRITUAL TEMPERATURE:

1   2   3   4   5   6   7   8   9   10

REFLECTIONS:

____

____

____

____

____

____

____

____

____

____

____

____

____

____

____

____

____

DATE: ____ DAY _______ OF MY CYCLE

SPIRITUAL TEMPERATURE:

1   2   3   4   5   6   7   8   9   10

REFLECTIONS:

____

____

____

____

____

____

____

____

____

____

____

____

____

____

DATE: _______________________________________ DAY _____ OF MY CYCLE

SPIRITUAL TEMPERATURE:

1   2   3   4   5   6   7   8   9   10

REFLECTIONS:

____

____

____

____

____

____

____

____

____

____

____

____

____

____

____

____

____

DATE: _________________________________ DAY _____ OF MY CYCLE

SPIRITUAL TEMPERATURE:

1   2   3   4   5   6   7   8   9   10

REFLECTIONS:

DATE: _________________________________ DAY _____ OF MY CYCLE

SPIRITUAL TEMPERATURE:

1   2   3   4   5   6   7   8   9   10

REFLECTIONS:

____

____

____

____

____

____

____

____

____

____

____

____

____

____

____

____

____

____

DATE: _______________________________ DAY _______ OF MY CYCLE

SPIRITUAL TEMPERATURE:

1   2   3   4   5   6   7   8   9   10

REFLECTIONS:

DATE: _______________________________ DAY _____ OF MY CYCLE

SPIRITUAL TEMPERATURE:

1   2   3   4   5   6   7   8   9   10

REFLECTIONS:

DATE: _______________________________________ DAY _____ OF MY CYCLE

SPIRITUAL TEMPERATURE:

1   2   3   4   5   6   7   8   9   10

REFLECTIONS:

____

____

____

____

____

____

____

____

____

____

____

____

____

____

____

DATE: _______________________________ DAY _____ OF MY CYCLE

SPIRITUAL TEMPERATURE:

1   2   3   4   5   6   7   8   9   10

REFLECTIONS:

____

____

____

____

____

____

____

____

____

____

____

____

____

____

____

____

DATE: _________________________________ DAY _____ OF MY CYCLE

SPIRITUAL TEMPERATURE:

1   2   3   4   5   6   7   8   9   10

REFLECTIONS:

DATE: _____________________________________ DAY ______ OF MY CYCLE

SPIRITUAL TEMPERATURE:

1   2   3   4   5   6   7   8   9   10

REFLECTIONS:

____

____

____

____

____

____

____

____

____

____

____

____

____

____

____

____

____

____

DATE: ____ DAY _______ OF MY CYCLE

SPIRITUAL TEMPERATURE:

1   2   3   4   5   6   7   8   9   10

REFLECTIONS:

____

____

____

____

____

____

____

____

____

____

____

____

____

____

DATE: _________________________________ DAY _____ OF MY CYCLE

SPIRITUAL TEMPERATURE:

1   2   3   4   5   6   7   8   9   10

REFLECTIONS:

____

____

____

____

____

____

____

____

____

____

____

____

____

____

____

____

____

DATE: _________________________________ DAY _____ OF MY CYCLE

SPIRITUAL TEMPERATURE:

1   2   3   4   5   6   7   8   9   10

REFLECTIONS:

____

____

____

____

____

____

____

____

____

____

____

____

____

____

____

____

DATE: _________________________________ DAY _____ OF MY CYCLE

SPIRITUAL TEMPERATURE:

1   2   3   4   5   6   7   8   9   10

REFLECTIONS:

____

____

____

____

____

____

____

____

____

____

____

____

____

____

____

____

DATE: _________________________________ DAY _____ OF MY CYCLE

SPIRITUAL TEMPERATURE:

1   2   3   4   5   6   7   8   9   10

REFLECTIONS:

____

____

____

____

____

____

____

____

____

____

____

____

____

____

____

____

____

DATE: _________________________________ DAY _____ OF MY CYCLE

SPIRITUAL TEMPERATURE:

1   2   3   4   5   6   7   8   9   10

REFLECTIONS:

____

____

____

____

____

____

____

____

____

____

____

____

____

____

____

____

____

Part IV

LOOK DEEPER

Go higher.

Go deeper.

Embody.

Grow.

Become.

Be woke.

LOOK DEEPER

In this part, I will share references in each chapter with helpful resources in case you want to look deeper.

KNOWLEDGE

COMMUNITY

Become a student of Mishkah University

VIDEOS

"Knowledge" by Dr. Hatem Al Haj:

> https://www.stationsofthetravelers.com/55/knowledge-a-data-placementbottomtitle-see-the-previous-chapter-for-the-explanation-of-isndata-toggletooltipdata-htmltrue-sup433-sup-a.html

"Definition of Tawheed" by Yasir Qhadi:

> https://www.youtube.com/watch?v=ixBQ3mNpgpA

'Introduction | Names of Allah Ep. 01 by Tahir Wyatt:

> https://www.youtube.com/watch?v=b-8Ihjg489o&list=PLRI-67hGN2r3Lb0xCcI-Mk9JjKwCs1-diw

"Ibn Taymiyyah's Aqidah Wasitiyyah" By Tahir Wyatt:

> https://www.youtube.com/playlist?list=PLRI67hGN2r3JMT-TRX3vJ_OcoHt1iMfQUk

BOOKS

"Stations of the Travelers: Manâzil as-Sâ'ireen" translation and foot-notes by Dr. Hatem Al Haj:

> https://www.amazon.com/Stations-Travelers-as-Sâireen-Hatem-al-Haj/dp/B08BG2MJSV/ref=tmm_pap_swatch_0?_encoding=UTF8&qid=1593024073&sr=8-4

"Explanation of the three fundamental principles of Islaam" by Muhammad ibn Saalih al Uthaymeen:

> https://www.kalamullah.com/Books/Explanation%20of%20the%20Three%20Fundamental%20Principles%20of%20Islaam.pdf

"A Commentary on the Creed of Imam al Tahawi" By Shaykh Salih al Fawzan:

> https://www.islamicbookstore.com/b12376.html

"The Way of Truth: A Poem of Creed and Manner" translated by John Newton Starling III:

> https://www.amazon.com/Way-Truth-Poem-Creed-Manner/dp/0692961275/ref=sr_1_4?qid=1661283440&refinements=p_27%3AJohn+Newton+Starling+III&s=books&sr=1-4

WEBSITE

"Where is Allah":

> https://hadithoftheday.com/where-is-allah/

WISDOM

VIDEOS

"Chapter of Wisdom" by Dr. Hatem Al Haj:

https://www.stationsofthetravelers.com/56/wisdom.html

"The Seerah of the Prophet Muhammed (Peace and Blessings be Upon Him)" by Shaykh Bilal Assaad:

https://www.youtube.com/watch?v=z6nONOS9yGQ-&list=PLOlaiHoIQfAgjZPZdk_RNUVFBlBSdzu4C

"Seerah of Prophet Muhammed" by Yasir Qadhi:

https://www.youtube.com/watch?v=VOUp3ZZ9t3A&list=PLAEA99D24CA2F9A8F&index=1

"Fiqh Of Worship" by Dr. Hatem Al Haj:

https://www.youtube.com/watch?v=DeQb1pR-8B24&list=PLERXZaggdbqRZce0XPksZ3kvGGkUbsGFA

"Can I be spiritual without religion?" with Tom Facchine:

https://youtu.be/gj06gltStH4

DOCUMENTARY

"Our Planet" by BBC Earth

PODCAST

"BBC Earth"

BOOKS

"Meeting Muhammed" by Dr. Omar Suleiman:

https://a.co/d/fMdUT8u

WEBSITE

"Sharia":

> https://yaqeeninstitute.org/read/sharia

SURRENDER

VIDEOS

"Chapter on Surrender" by Dr. Hatem Al Haj:

> https://www.stationsofthetravelers.com/33/surrender-a-data-placementbottomtitle-pertinent-also-are-the-following-terms:-submit-give-up-give-in-hand-over-defer-renounce-data-toggletooltipdata-htmltrue-sup276-sup-a.html

"Road to Return" by Yahya Ibrahim:

> https://yaqeeninstitute.org/yahyaibrahim/ep-1-submitting-to-god-road-to-return

BOOKS

"Jami' Al-'Ulum Wa' L-Hikam" by Ibn Rajab:

> https://www.kalamullah.com/Books/collection%20of%20ilm.pdf

MANIFESTATION

VIDEOS

"If God is Merciful, Why Does Hellfire Exist?" with Sh. Mohamed Elshinawy:

> https://www.youtube.com/watch?v=XD6NjaCxEZE

"Why Allah Allows Earthquakes and Suffering" with Dr. Omar Suleiman:

> https://www.youtube.com/watch?v=vB7tA6yKwdY&t=1s

"Why didn't God stop it?" with Mohammed Elshinawi:

> https://youtu.be/B1L6j6XvHT0

BOOKS

"Dua | The weapon of the believer" by Abu Ammaar Yasir Qadhi:

> https://www.kalamullah.com/Books/Dua%20The%20Weapon%20Of%20The%20Believer.pdf

WEBSITE

"Reconciling the Divine Decree and Free Will in Islam" by Justin Parrot:

> https://yaqeeninstitute.org/read/paper/reconciling-the-divine-decree-and-free-will-in-islam

"Conscious or Coerced: Divine Decree in Islam" By Yaqeen Institute:

> https://yaqeeninstitute.org/curriculum/principles-of-faith/divine-decree-in-islam

INSPIRATION

VIDEOS

"Inspiration" by Dr. Hatem Al Haj:

> https://www.stationsofthetravelers.com/60/inspiration.html

"Sciences of the Quran" by Yasir Qadhi:

> https://www.youtube.com/watch?v=voMjhfEBRO4&list=PLACEB19198355B61C

BOOKS

"Angels in Your Presence" by Dr. Omar Suleiman:

> https://a.co/d/39xM4eJ

WEBSITE

"Do you really Believe in Angels? | In Pursuit of Conviction" By Dr. Zohair Abdul-Rahman:

https://yaqeeninstitute.org/read/paper/in-pursuit-of-conviction-iii-do-you-really-believe-in-angels

MENTAL ASTUTENESS

BOOKS

"WomanCode" by Alisa Vitti:

https://a.co/d/d4iYZdU

WEBSITE

Robin Nelson:

https://naturalhormonesolution.com

ARTICLES

Herrando C, Constantinides E. Emotional Contagion: "A Brief Overview and Future Directions."

Front Psychol. 2021 Jul 16;12:712606. doi: 10.3389/fpsyg.2021.712606. PMID: 34335425; PMCID: PMC8322226.

SPIRITUAL ASTUTENESS

VIDEOS

"Chapter on Astuteness" by Dr. Hatem Al Haj:

https://www.stationsofthetravelers.com/58/astuteness-a-data-placementbottomtitle-firsah-is-about-the-power-of-good-prediction-the-possessor-of-this-quality-can-tell-people-apart-from-their-conduct-and-may-be-able-to-see-what-others-may-not-thereby-predicting-what-they-cannot-sometimes-it-is-through-the-exquisite-ability-to-detect-subtle-signals-but-what-the-sheikh-is-addressing-here-is-mainly-that-which-results-from-inspiration-or-disclosure-data-toggletooltipdata-htmltrue-sup459-sup-a.html

BOOKS

"Ranks of the Divine Seekers" (Madarij al- Salikin) by Ibnul Qayyim al Jawziyyah:

https://www.kalamullah.com/madarij-al-salikin.html

THE STATE OF ABUNDANCE

VIDEOS

"Gratefulness" by Dr. Hatem Al Haj:

https://www.stationsofthetravelers.com/36/gratefulness.html

WEBSITE

"The Divine Gift Of Gratitude" by Sarah Sultan:

https://yaqeeninstitute.org/read/paper/the-divine-gift-of-gratitude-the-secret-of-happiness-in-the-modern-world

"Giving Thanks Can Make You Happier":

https://www.health.harvard.edu/healthbeat/giving-thanks-can-make-you-happier

"The Art Of Gratitude" by Dr. Tamer Desouky:

https://yaqeeninstitute.org/read/paper/the-art-of-gratitude-quranic-themes-on-shukr

BLINDERS

VIDEOS

"Social Media is making me Jealous- Part 1":

> https://www.youtube.com/watch?v=1Mk75ugXt_0&t=2s

"Social Media is making me Jealous- Part 2":

> https://youtu.be/v7kQ6zKNnSY

"How to Control Anger" by Yasir Qadhi:

> https://www.youtube.com/watch?v=1HwjkcDFy6Y

"Secrets of the Heart" by Sh. Moutasem Al-Hameedi:

> https://www.youtube.com/playlist?list=PLVI8matu_Br0KUm9BKb1WkX8S_53YtzFt

"OCD and Satan's Whispers" with Sr. Najwa Awad:

> https://youtu.be/utpnE1_Gzks

BOOKS

"The Body Keeps the Score: Brain, Mind, and Body in the Healing of Trauma" by Bessel van der Kolk:

> https://a.co/d/gmVP8e4

"Boundary Boss: The Essential Guide to Talk True, Be Seen, and (Finally) Live Free" by Terri Cole:

> https://a.co/d/bUyWK5C

"Healing The Child Within: Discovery and Recovery for Adult Children of Dysfunctional Families" by Charles L. Whitfield M.D.:

> https://a.co/d/0glKbJu

WEBSITE

> https://www.traumahealingaccelerated.com
>
> https://www.healthline.com/human-body-maps/vagus-nerve

"Your Lord has not forsaken you" by Sarah Sultan and Najwa Awad:

> https://yaqeeninstitute.org/read/paper/your-lord-has-not-forsaken-you-addressing-the-impact-of-trauma-on-faith

"What Did I Do to Deserve This?" by Najwa Awad and Sarah Sultan:

> https://yaqeeninstitute.org/read/paper/what-did-i-do-to-deserve-this-conquering-the-assumptions-that-hold-you-back

THE PLEDGE OF THE WOKE WRITER

VIDEOS

"Spiritual Training" by Dr. Hatem Al Haj:

> https://www.stationsofthetravelers.com/13/training.html

"Habits to Win Here and Hereafter" with Dr. Tesneem Alkiek:

> https://yaqeeninstitute.org/tesneem-alkiek/ep1-know-your-purpose-habits-to-win-here-and-hereafter

BOOKS

"Between the God of the Prophets and the God of the Philosophers: Reflections of an Athari on the Divine Attributes" By Dr. Hatem Al Haj:

> https://a.co/d/esGKr9K

GATHERING THE TROOPS

BOOKS

"Purification of the Heart and Soul (Illness & Cure)" by Imam Ibn Qayyim al Jawziyyah:

> https://a.co/d/6dtTfs5

Atlas of the Heart by Brene Brown:

> https://a.co/d/dEeU8ZB

THE WOKE WRITER

COMMUNITIES

The Writers Block By Strange Inc.:

Strange incorporated.org

Women's Fiction Writers Association (WFWA)

BOOKS

"The War of Art" by Steven Pressfield:

https://a.co/d/cT5WEap

"Intuitive Editing" by Tiffany Yates Martin:

https://a.co/d/ga02oqK

"Dear Writer: You Need to Quit" by Rebecca Syme:

https://a.co/d/34yQQBu

"Save the Cat Writes a Novel" by Jessica Brody:

https://a.co/d/8IrWF2v

WEBSITES

Writing Mastery Academy (Founded by Jessica Brody):

https://www.writingmastery.com

PODCASTS

"Helping Writers Become Authors" by KM Weiland:

https://www.helpingwritersbecomeauthors.com/podcasts/

"The Strange Inc. Show | For Muslim Women Writers":

https://podcasters.spotify.com/pod/show/strangeinc

IMPORTANT TERMS

Our Big Why

> Our ultimate purpose in life is to worship Allah, who created us.

Our Small Why

> This is the how in our Big Why. It is how we use what Allah has given us to work toward living our ultimate purpose, which is to worship Allah.

Fitra

> A state which we were born in, which is an inner moral compass. It is our natural disposition and inclination toward good.

Rayada

> Spiritual training

Husnuthun billah

> To think good of Allah

Tawheed Ar Rububiyyah

> To know Allah through Allah's actions which show His Lordship such as sustaining everything and creating everything

Tawheed Ul Ulhiyyah

To know Allah through our actions of worshipping Him

Tawheed Al Asma Wasifat

To know Allah through His names and attributes which were revealed in the Quran and the Sunnah

Sunnah

The way of the final Messenger ﷺ

Baseera

From the Arabic word *Basr* which means sight. *Baseera* is insight.

Hikmah

From the Arabic word *Hakm* which means everything in its proper place. *Hikmah* is wisdom.

Dhulm

Literal meaning in Arabic is something in the wrong place. *Dhulm* is transgression and injustice.

Ilm

Knowledge

Hilm

Forbearance. This means when our emotions are expressed in a healthy and balanced way without extremes of repressing them or overexpressing them.

Adl

Justice

Anaa

Deliberation

Qadr

The Decree of Allah

Shariah

Literal meaning in Arabic is "a path to water." *Shariah* is the body of Islamic law from the Quran and the way of the final Messenger ﷺ.

Kitaab

Literal meaning in Arabic is "book". In terms of Allah's Decree, it means the writing of the decrees in the different books of decree.

Al Lawh Al Mahfooz

Also known as The Mother of All Books and the Preserved Tablet. All the decrees have been written here and they are based on Allah's perfect knowledge. They are unchangeable.

Laylatul Qadr

The night of decree which is in the last ten days of Ramadan. The decrees for the next year are written for each of us and this decree can be changed through making Dua (supplication).

Dua

Asking Allah for anything we want

Ilham

Inspiration. It encompasses all kinds of inspiration such as true dreams, understanding of something, and so on.

Ahlul sunnah wal Jammah

The way of the majority who follow our final Messenger ﷺ

Muhadith

A person who has received the highest kind of inspiration, below *Wahy*. Unlike *Wahy*, this inspiration has room for error.

Wahy

This is inspiration which is sent to the prophets and messengers and it has no room for error.

Firasa

Spiritual and mental astuteness. It means to see people at a deeper level with insight.

Mujiza

Miracles sent only to the prophets and messengers so the people could find resolve in their call to Allah.

Karamat

Miracles sent to those Allah has chosen who are not prophets or messengers. These miracles are only for them and not to be shown off to the people.

Biddah

An unpraiseworthy kind of addition to the religion

Shaytan

The Devil

Ihsaan

Excellence

Kufr

To bury the seed of faith, to disbelieve

Shukr

To show thanks to Allah through our heart, tongue, and limbs

Qalb

Literal meaning in Arabic is to turn. *Qalb* refers to the heart.

Birr

Righteousness and good works

Ithm

Sin and transgression

ACKNOWLEDGEMENTS

I am grateful to Allah for blessing me to write this book. To my parents: my mother a symbol of strength; my father, who nurtured my imagination through telling me stories about our prophets in a way which shaped my understanding of true superheroes.

I am also grateful to and for my husband who has constantly reminded me of who I am and my children who have helped me take off the layers of my own blinders, as only children can. I hope they find solace in these words after I am gone.

I am grateful to my sister, Maryam, who also happens to be my Irish twin. She has been my gateway to Islam for as long as I can remember, always nurturing and supporting me, whilst exemplifying what it means to be a beautiful human being. I am grateful to both my brothers, Naqeeb, straight talking but sobering in his support, so when he said he believed in Strange Inc., I knew he meant it. And Hamzah who serves as my reminder of thoughtfulness, kindness and compassion. Our conversations about writing were always wholesome, and I hope to one day read his novel.

I am grateful to all the board members of Strange Inc.. Each of you has helped me think in new ways, and each of you has been a pillar of strength for me in your own beautiful way.

I am also grateful to my editor, Laura El Alam, who, when she learnt of this project, was excited. Her words motivated me to challenge myself to finally finish this book. It takes a team to write a book and I am grateful to and for my talented designer Alexandra Sieh who has been a pleasure to work with. She reminded me of the good in people and how beautiful the world can really be.

I am grateful to my school, Mishkah University, where I have been learning since the emergence of The Strangers in 2014, which I don't believe is coincidental. Anytime I have felt I needed clarity, I have been blessed with some amazing teachers and fellow students.

The greatest teachers are the ones who show us ourselves, and Dr. Hatem Al Haj did this without even knowing. His lessons and his advice have changed my life, and until this day, I remember the depth of three short words which he said to me: "Follow Your Heart." It was then I began to understand that we each have a Small Why, and it is unique to us. Islam honors our identity, and when we do things for Allah, we will never lose.

I am grateful to you, my reader, my sister, and my soul friend, who has been on this journey with me. Who read these words and put meaning to them in your own life. May Allah bless all of you, in this life and the next. May Allah always guide us upon the straight path. Ameen.

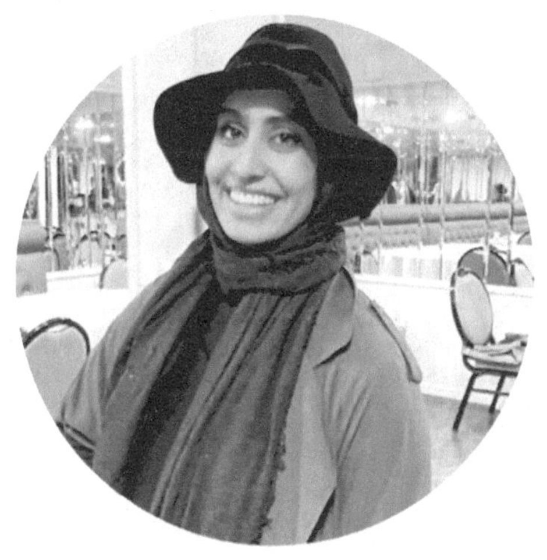

ABOUT THE AUTHOR

Aishah Alam lives in New York with her two hobbit-resembling daughters and her husband who happens to love boots vigorously. She was born in Leeds, UK, where she grew up enjoying her visits to the library and eating Sara Lee Chocolate Gateau, which unfortunately have been discontinued. After moving to New York in 2011, she founded Strange Incorporated in 2014, then known as The Strangers, a nonprofit grassroots poetry movement which gave platform to the youth to express their faith eloquently. Strange Inc. is now a nonprofit publishing house and embodies Aishah's mission, which is to elevate the authentic voices of Muslim women. She also has a social work degree and has just completed her bachelor's degree in Islamic Studies with Mishkah University.

ABOUT STRANGE INC.

Strange Inc. is dedicated to empowering Muslim women's voices worldwide. With a faith-based approach and a commitment to truthfulness and excellence, they unite creatives, using art to heal and reclaim identities. Through publications, writing shows, and support groups, they strive to amplify authentic voices and dispel misrepresentations. Their unwavering mission is to promote religious freedom, integrity, and cultural expression. Learn more at www.strangeincorporated.org.

ENDNOTES

1   Ibn Taymiyyah, The Refutation of the Contradiction of
    Reason and Revelation
2   Quran, Surah Araf, verse 172
3   Between the God of the Prophets and the God of the
    Philosophers: Reflections of an Athari on the Divine
    Attributes by Dr. Hatem Al Haj
4   Sahih Al Bukhari
5   Tawheed Ar rububiyyah
6   Tawheed al ulhiyyah
7   Tawheed al asma wasifat
8   Baseera
9   Husntuhun billah
10 Ibnul Qayyim al Jawziyyah spoke of three of these:
    Knowledge, forbearance and deliberation in Madharij
    As Salikeen
11 Al-Adab al-Mufrad 1322
12 This is not in the original three pillars of wisdom by Ibnul
    Qayyim al Jawziyyah; it was added by Dr. Hatem Al Haj
13 Dr. Hatem Al Haj
14 Sahih Muslim
15 Sunan al-Tirmidhii

16   Sahih Al Bukhari

17   Sahih Al Bukhari

18   Sahih Al Bukhari

19   Inna lillahi wainna illayhi rajioon

20   Birr is the expansion of the chest due to righteousness and Ithm is the tightness of the chest from sin

21   The Chaos Theory

22   Quran, Surah Al Anam, verse 59

23   Quran, Surah Araf, verse 172

24   Al Lawh Al Mahfooz

25   Quran, Surah Hajj, verse 70

26   Al Lawh Al Mahfooz

27   Al-Bukhari and Muslim

28   Laylatul Qadr

29   Al Bukhari and Muslim

30   Irrada Kawniya

31   Irrada Shariah

32   Quran, Az Zumar, verse 62

33   Quran, Surah Ghafir, verse 60

34   Quran, Surah Ibrahim, verse 7

35   Quran, Surah Al Isra, verse 81

36   Quran, At Tahrim, verse 11

37   Quran, Surah Al Baqara, verse 23

38   Quran, Surah Al Anfal, verse 29

39   A good hadeeth transmitted from the musnads of the two imams, Ahmed bin Hambal and Al- Darimi, with a good chain of authorities.

40   The Ahlul sunnah wal Jammah

41   Sahih Muslim

42   Musnad of Imam Ahmed

43   In the companion course, we referred to this as "prediction"

44   Firasa

45   Sunan al-Tirmidhī 3127

46   Quran, Surah Hijr, verse 75

47   Rayaada

48 Narrated by Ahmad in Fadaa'il al-Sahaabah

49 Awliyah

50 A being who is unseen and made from smokeless fire

51 Sahih Al Bukhari

52 Wahy

53 An unpraiseworthy innovation which has no roots in the Quran and the Sunnah or the pious predecessors

54 Al-Silsilah al-Saheehah

55 Dr. Hatem Al Haj

56 Iblis

57 Quran, Surah ArRaf, verse 17

58 The testimony of faith, praying five times a day, giving Zakat, making the pilgrimage Hajj (if we can) and fasting during Ramadan (if we can)

59 Al Bukhari

60 All Praise to Allah

61 The Devil

62 Ihya ulum al-din by al-Ghazali

63 Abu Hamid Al-Ghazali

64 Quran, Surah Al Hashr, verse 10

65 Gabor Mate

66 Quran, Surah Al Baqara, verse 283

67 Discipline, The Path of Spiritual Growth By Imam Ibn Qaudamah al-maqdisi

68 Ihsaan

69 Narrated by Ibn 'Abd al-Barr in Jaami' Bayaan al-'Ilm wa Fadluhu

70 Sunan of Ibn Majah, Hasan

71 Quran, Surah Rahman, verse 60